Two wo

Educating Africa's youth for rural development

Other publications of the Bernard van Leer Foundation

1971 *Compensatory early childhood education*
A selective working bibliography

1972 *Early childhood education in Jamaica*
A project monograph

1972 *Early childhood education in the Caribbean*
A seminar report

1974 *Curriculum in early childhood education*
A seminar report

Educating Africa's youth for rural development

Archibald Callaway

Bernard van Leer Foundation

Published in 1974 by the Bernard van Leer Foundation

ISBN 90 6195 005 8

The authors' views are not necessarily those of the Bernard van Leer Foundation, and the designations employed and the presentation of the material do not imply the expression of any opinion whatsoever on the part of the Foundation concerning the legal status of any country or territory, or of its authorities, or concerning the delimitations of the frontiers of any country or territory.

Photographs are reproduced by kind permission of the Ministry of Education of the Western State & of the North-Central State, Nigeria (1-12); of Sandy Grant, Gaberones, Botswana (13 and 14); and of the Ministry of Education, Sierra Leone (15).

The author wishes to thank Mr. Lester James of the University of Manchester for his help in designing the chart.

Design by Tel Design Associated
Printed in the Netherlands
Drukkerij Verweij, Mijdrecht

Contents

Foreword

The Bernard van Leer Foundation, created for broad humanitarian purposes, for almost ten years has been supporting activities aimed at enabling children and youth throughout schoolgoing age, who are impeded by the social and cultural inadequacy of their background and environment, to achieve the greatest possible realisation of their total potential.

To attain this end the Foundation has helped to set up a network of experimental projects in about twenty countries all over the world from which exchanges of project experience are taking place and multiplication models are being developed.
Inevitably the Foundation's sphere of activities demands study of the special needs of the young as determined by the social and economic characteristics of particular areas. The present publication on problems confronting rural youth in tropical Africa and possible solutions represents the first such undertaking by the Foundation. The study is limited in geographical scope and thus does not include all African countries in which the Foundation is active.

The Foundation is indebted to Professor Archibald Callaway for having brought his wealth of knowledge and experience of the African scene to bear on the problems of its rural youth.

Summary

From 70 to 90 per cent of today's boys and girls in tropic African nations are growing up in the rural areas. They are t sons and daughters of farmers, herdsmen, fishermen, and also rural transporters, traders, and craftsmen. Some of these you people will gain further education and work in the cities. A fe with specialist training will obtain rural wage-paid jobs as tract drivers, as clerks in local cooperatives, or as extension agen

But the great majority will have to find their life vocations self-employed rural producers. They will work within characte istic small-scale enterprises through the countryside, in the present home localities or in other villages or rural towns.

Governments are faced with seemingly intractable problems determining how best to intervene (a) to provide appropria education and (b) to expand the work opportunities available f rural youth.

The capacity of any particular nation to meet these twin obje tives depends, in large measure, on the pace and direction economic development. What has become increasingly evide during the past decade is that some nations are in a much mo favourable position than others to educate and employ you people. Zambia, Gabon, Nigeria, with substantial revenu generated from mineral exports, for example, are better able assist their younger generations than are Ethiopia, Somal Chad, Mali, Mauritania, Niger, where the dynamic for develo ment deriving from exports is much less.

What kinds of education are rural boys and girls in these cou tries now receiving? How do these relate to rural developme In what ways can such education be improved?

In educating young people for future rural occupations, there a three main approaches: on-the-job-training; schooling; traini courses.

a the Koranic School

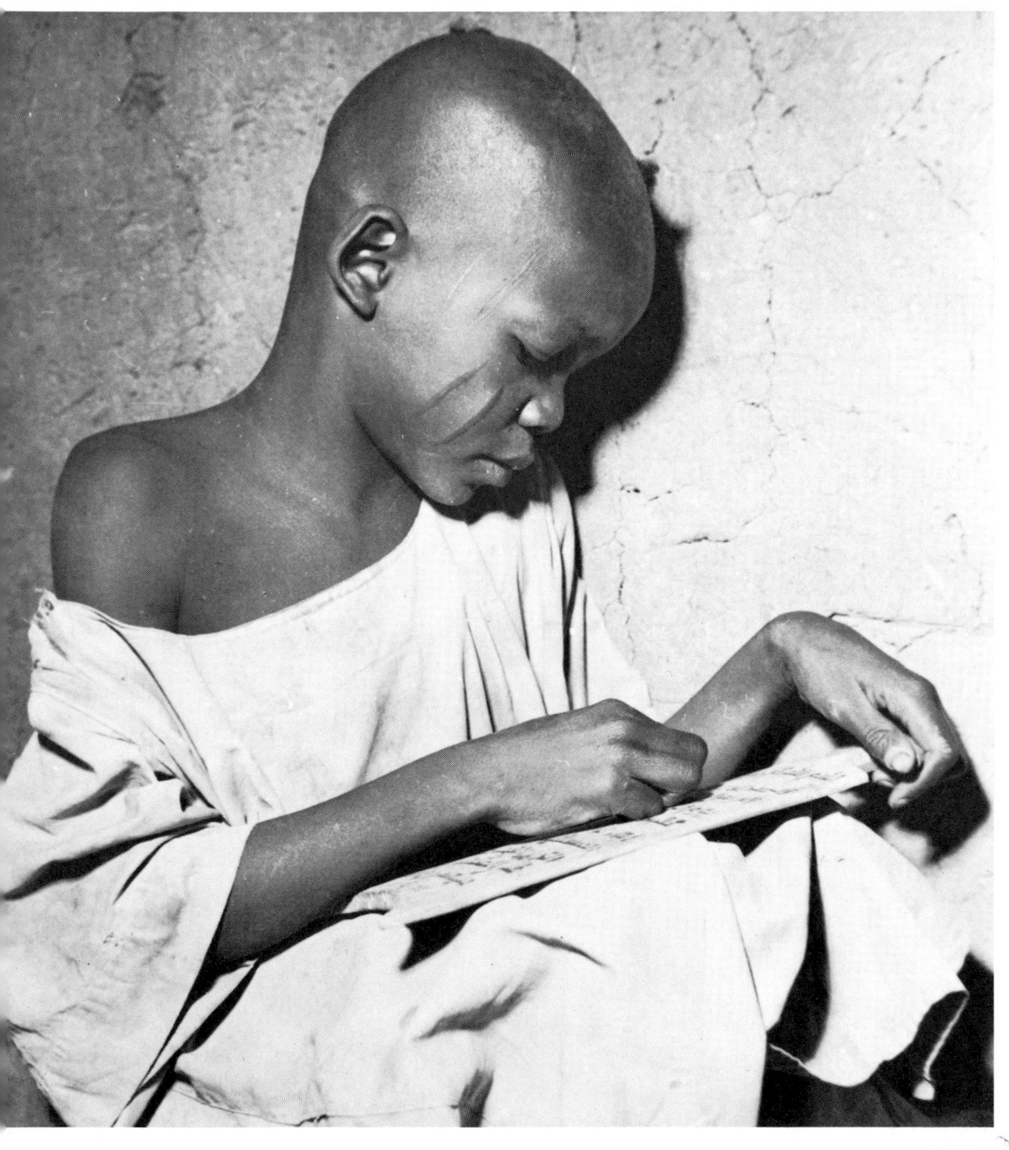

2
Story telling carries on cultural traditions

he Koranic School

4
Children playing a local game with a snail shell

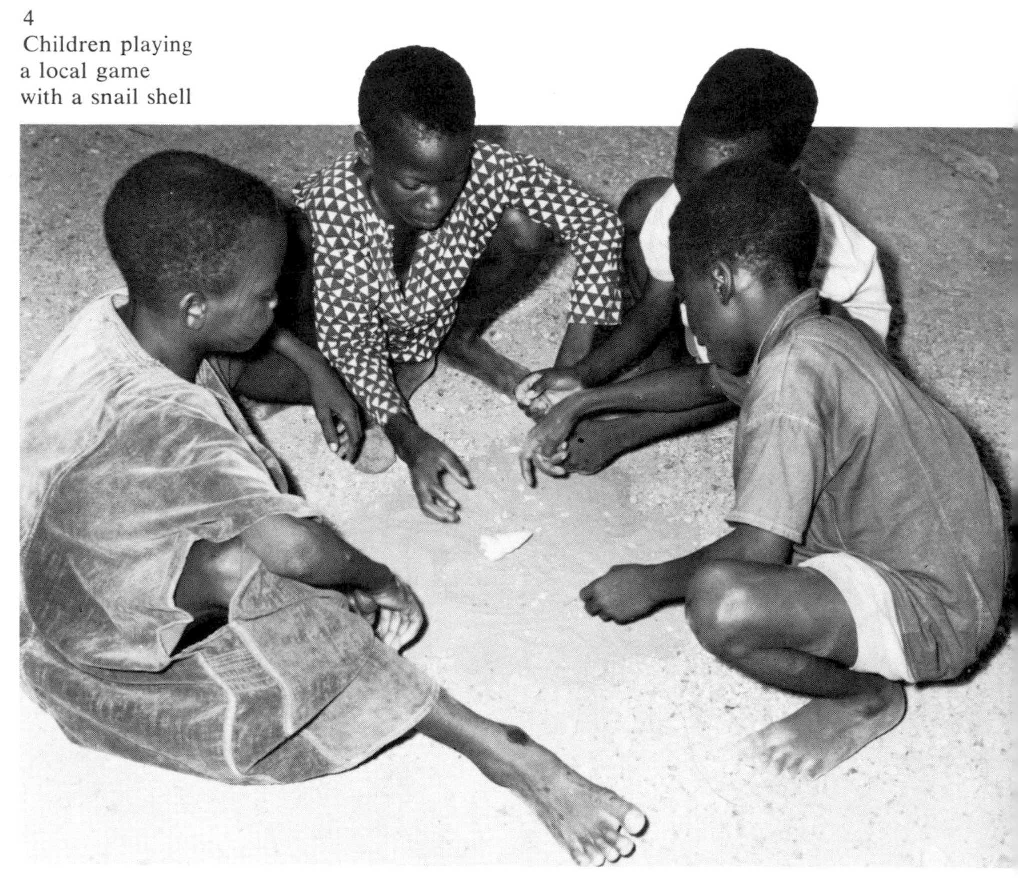

On-the-job training

Experience and everyday perception emphasize that the most valid way to become a farmer or a trader or a craftsmen is to learn on the job from those actively at work. This is the case whether a youth is a primary school leaver, a dropout from the local school, or has not been to school at all.

Such vocational learning on the job is part of indigenous learning processes by which societies pass on from one generation to the next their cultural heritage – not only of their rituals and religion, art and oral literature, social values, health care and nutrition, but also their technical skills.

The nature of indigenous education varies greatly from one society to another, depending on social customs and the ways people manage their economic environment. In areas of extreme economic hardship children may suffer from severe malnutrition and gain only rudimentary skills from impoverished parents. In other instances, children have balanced diets and learn occupations through structured programmes of apprenticeship.

Vocational training generally begins early, often by the age of 7 or 8, when the child accompanies an adult to the workplace – whether farm, market, or workshop – to learn by observing, listening, imitating, and gradually taking a more responsible part in work activities.

What is clear is that parents and other adults cannot pass on to youth skills that they do not themselves possess. It follows that whatever is done through programmes of extension services (supported by varied media such as demonstrations and the use of radio and print in local languages) to widen the knowledge and improve the work performances of adults in farm skills, health, or community development will benefit young people.

These extension programmes thus have a significant multiplier effect.

The second approach in educating rural children is through th school. Dissatisfaction with formal schooling is often voiced: tha it creates an unnecessarily sharp break with local realities. Whil the main cause of school leavers' employment problem can b attributed to the slow-moving rural economic environment, contributing factor may well be cited that schooling is not suffi ciently related to indigenous learning processes.

Although proportions attending primary schools vary consider ably among nations and within zones in any one nation, a overall figure for the 35 nations of tropical Africa shows onl about 30 per cent of rural children presently in school. While al these nations (taken here as coincident with the administrativ area of UNESCO's regional office) have endorsed the goal o universal primary education, lack of financial resources togethe with rapidly increasing populations make the achievement o such an ideal, for most of them, out of reach in the near future This study examines the possibilities for reducing education cost and thus making it feasible for more children to attend school for the same outlay in public expenditures. The complexities o the problem are also analysed of how to make the schoo experience more relevant to rural life and work.

The third approach in educating rural youth is through trainin courses in such diverse topics as health and child care, poultry keeping, or technical operations of making concrete blocks o creating fishponds. These may be designed for school leavers o for those with little or no schooling. They may take place in th classroom of a training centre or in the field as a combination o study and work. They may be introduced as part of social group ings such as young farmers' clubs, young women's associations or as features of comprehensive land settlement projects.

Much of the success of intervening in this way (by central an local governments and voluntary organizations) depends, how ever, on recognition of the central significance of on-the-jo training. Experience during the 1960s shows that lengthy post-primary courses (provided at some age beyond school leaving) have had good results in preparing rural youth for wage-paid jobs. But for the greater numbers who will become self-employed rural producers, success has been greater with short courses, provided intermittently, and thus not disrupting the process of learning on the job.

A critical issue of the past decade has been that whatever education is provided for rural youth, their chances for self-improvement later will be marginal unless there is a wider framework for promoting rural development. The earlier obsession with devoting an exceptionally high proportion of public funds and administrative talent to capital-intensive projects – which, especially in the case of industries, are usually clustered in cities – has led to excessive numbers of rural youth migrating in order to compete for the relatively few wage-paid jobs. As a result, many have remained without jobs for long periods.

More emphasis will now have to be given to strategies for labour-intensity, both in improving agriculture and in setting up rural industries. The task facing governments is formidable. For one thing there are logistic difficulties of communicating with distant rural families. For another, there are usually insufficient numbers of trained extension workers and support personnel. And it is evident, too, that the most economic and effective methods for stimulating rural advancement have not yet been evolved for local use.

The aim is to strengthen the productivity of small-scale economic units throughout the rural areas. When this happens more substantive learning situations will be created for rural youth, on the job.

Growing up in rural communities

1 Children and youth in their rural setting

The overwhelming proportion of families in the nations o tropical Africa live in the rural areas. Within wide stretches o the countryside and within particular cultures, many rural child- ren are at a severe disadvantage. Compared with children i urban centres, they have on the average less access to moder education and medical care, less prospect for self-improvement less chance of working themselves out of poverty during thei own lifetimes. (While children of some migrant and other fami- lies living precariously in cities grow up in equally adverse cir- cumstances, they usually have greater opportunities for educa- tion; and, in any case, the numbers of rural children are muc higher.) It is in the rural zones of tropical rainforest, o savannah, of desert, among the scattered farms and grazin tracts, that the more extreme difficulties are encountered i attempting to generate a more vital and relevant education fo young people and, at the same time, to create an improved en- vironment for their future work and living.

Poor health has been a central factor in perpetuating rural im- poverishment from one generation to the next. Lack of balance nutrition, susceptibility to diseases, contaminated water supplie – these are the conditions which drain the energies of adults cause high rates of infant mortality, and inhibit the mental an physical growth of children who survive. It is true that thes health deficiencies have long been recognized and during the pas few decades effective measures have been taken by nationa governments, international organizations, and voluntary agencies

In many areas smallpox, measles, and polio are no longer th threatening diseases of a generation ago; malaria is graduall being eradicated. Maternity clinics and hospitals are being set u outside urban districts. Clean water supplies are for the first tim available at some village sites. Yet even with this effort, vas territories still have virtually no modern medical facilities and perhaps equally important, no encouragement for improvin family nutrition and household sanitation.

Children under the age of 15 at present comprise about half the total populations of the nations in tropical Africa. Three-quarters of these boys and girls belong to rural families. With such large – and rapidly rising – numbers of young people, governments are confronted with acute problems in arranging improved opportunities for their education and productive work. Universal primary education is an objective supported by all nations of tropical Africa. But most countries will not be able to achieve such widespread schooling for the next decade; while for some countries this may not be attainable by the end of the century.

Although systems of formal education have been rapidly expanded by a number of countries during the 1960s, even so less than 40 per cent of school-age children in tropical Africa now attend primary schools. This proportion falls far short of the targets accepted at the Addis Ababa conference of 1961: of 70 per cent in schools by 1970, 100 per cent by 1980. This aggregate, of course, does not show the wide variations among nations, among different areas within nations, or between urban districts and rural. Who are the children *not* in school? Among some nomads or settled farming families in thinly-populated territories, no children at all go to school; while in many cities and urban regions, 90 per cent or more of school-age children are learning to read and write in an organized setting. These are the extremes. *Of normal school-age children throughout tropical Africa, some 70 per cent are not attending primary schools and thus are not gaining the skills of literacy and numeracy.*

In creating more places in schools to meet the increasing school-age populations, a central difficulty has been finance. Budgets of central and local governments have become strained, with high proportions of available funds devoted to formal schooling in order to pay for the training and salaries of teachers and for educational administration. At the same time, far-reaching discussions have been taking place on the relevance of formal schooling and the quality of education imparted: on curriculur content, technologies used, and methods of instruction. D present-day schools provide learning consistent with local real ties and with national objectives for development? In particula schools in rural areas often appear to create excessive disconti nuities with community life. As a consequence of the sluggish ness of the local economy (and perhaps, in some measure, be cause of the inappropriate school experience), numbers of rura school leavers migrate to towns and cities where they ofte remain for long periods without jobs. The employment difficul ties of school leavers are particularly obvious for those aged fi teen and upwards.

– *Vast numbers of rural children not gaining primary education.*
– *High costs of expanding school systems.*
– *Lack of relevance of primary school curricula.*
– *Widespread unemployment among school leavers.*

These problems affecting the future lives of millions of Africa children – expressed vividly in French-speaking Africa as *'l'im passe scolaire'* – have forced the revaluation of old ideas an the consideration of new lines of thinking.
– *How can many more children be brought into schools?*
– *How can unit costs be lowered?*
– *Can rural schools be made more relevant to rural work an living while strengthening the central objectives of literacy an numeracy?*
– *How can economic growth be encouraged throughout 'bus areas' (as seen from capital cities) so that rural incomes are in creased and new productive ventures create more jobs?*
– *Can designs for education be widened?*

This last question has focussed attention on an important bu neglected side of education: the learning activities which go o outside schools. Too often education is thought of institutionall that business which takes place in schools and shows its resul in diplomas and certificates. To deride this narrow idea c education does not imply that schools should be abolished (as some reformers now appear to suggest) but rather that greater recognition be given to the vital strands of learning going on outside the school.

Any review of the education requirements of Africa's rural children must begin by exploring the situation that now exists, including a careful appraisal of out-of-school learning or the millions of children not attending primary schools, what learning activities do they take part in? What educative influences are they exposed to in their families, communities, work-places? How do they get the training to become adult workers? And for primary school leavers, what lines of vocational training are available to improve their practical skills, whether in classrooms or on the job?

These many and varied forms of out-of-school education can be classified as:
Processes of learning that are part of the fabric of rural society,
Programmes of out-of-school education originating with central and local governments or voluntary organizations, and
Projects for development, with a specific geographic location, which include education in one form or another.

The indigenous learning *processes* of a rural society provide the means for passing on from one generation to the next its cultural heritage of rituals and religion, art and oral literature, social values, technologies, economic skills. While some societies are relatively unchanging, others are adapting quickly to new values and ways of doing things and thus provide new patterns for raising their children. In this context it is important to view education as a continuum through the entire lifecycle, starting with birth and continuing through infancy, pre-school, school, adolescence, and adulthood. Children grow up in families and in communities; they learn from parents and other adults, from their contemporaries, from individuals and from group experience.

They learn by observing, listening, imitating and taking pa in activities. It is evident that education which improves th knowledge and work practices of adults becomes part of th patterns transmitted to young people.

Programmes of education, set up by central or local governmen or generated locally by voluntary organizations or by the con munities themselves, supplement these forms of customary lear ing. These include practical courses or special assistance i agricultural improvement, nutrition and child-care, communi development practices – provided chiefly by the extension se vices of governments. Literacy classes come under this categor Clearly, these programmes can be successful only to the exte that the indigenous society and its customary processes of lear ing are examined and understood.

Specific development *projects,* which include some forms c education, may also be initiated by governments or communiti themselves. Some are for creating infrastructure (access road dams, wells); others are for starting small industries, farm settl ments, irrigation schemes. Although some of these projects i clude only a few participants and are contained geographicall there is usually a built-in hope that the results can be diffuse over a wider area.

Primary schools in many areas create an unnecessarily sha break with rural life; pupils gain attitudes and aspirations whic have little chance of being fulfilled in their home setting. I contrast, out-of-school learning is more often closely aligned rural social and economic activities. Continuity and gradu change are its characteristics. But these seeming polarities are fact only points on a graduated scale. Educational policies ca be devised to encourage primary schooling more in line wi local realities and, at the same time, to infuse out-of-scho education with greater dynamics. Such policies, however, ha their effect only within the context of rural improvement. Educ

ithmetic class in
village school

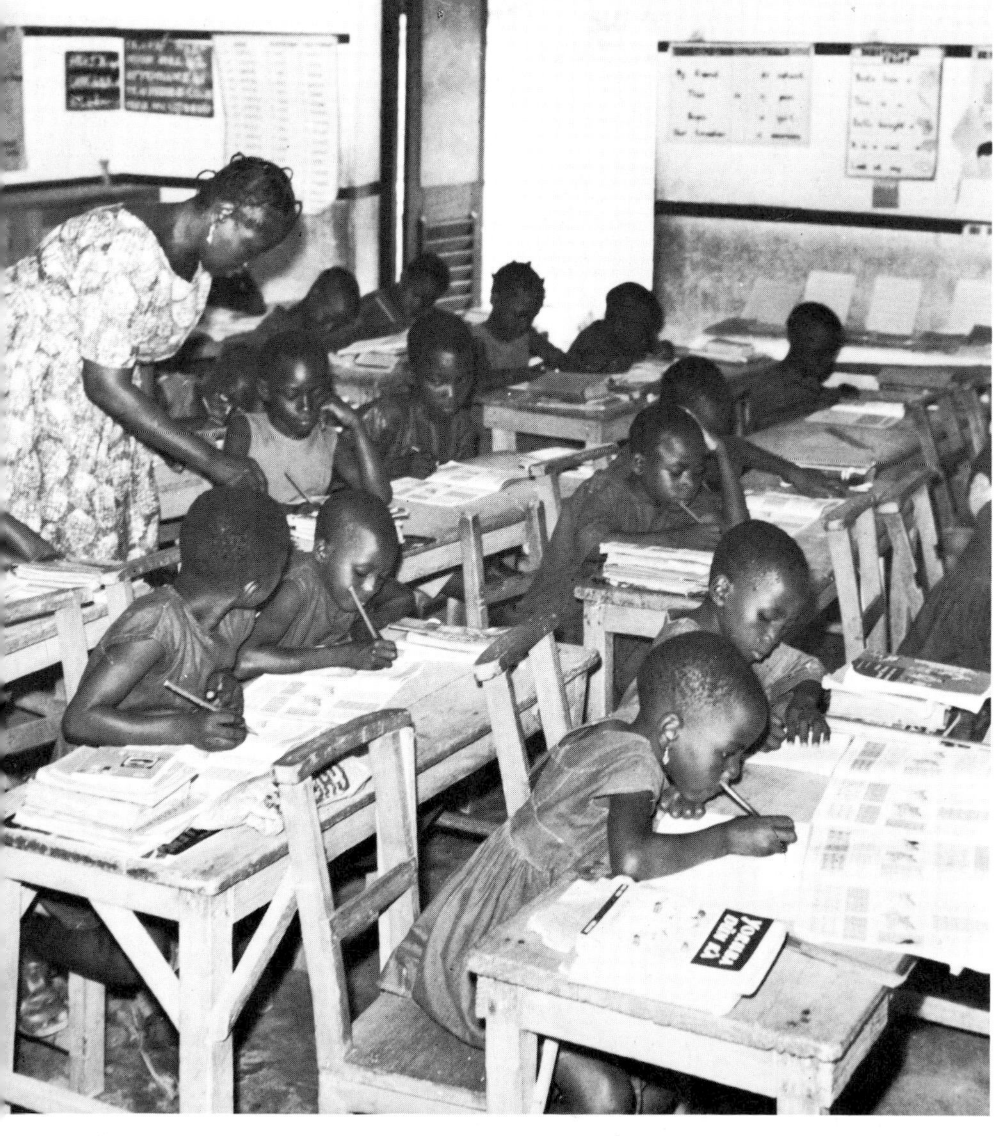

6
Returning home from the village primary school

tion of any kind, whether provided inside or outside classrooms, cannot yield its full potentialities in changing the lives of rural young people unless closely allied to better opportunities for work.

It is the purpose of this paper to analyse these problems of disadvantaged rural youth in tropical Africa and, in tracing the interrelationships of various types of education with one another and with the economy, to outline policy suggestions for education and rural development.

High rates of population increase

The *levels* of population in individual nations of tropical Africa are not excessive. The ratio of population to arable land, for example, is broadly favourable. Most nations, in fact, might be defined as underpopulated because they have empty cultivable land and because widely-spread populations mean high per capita costs for public utilities and administration. It is not over-population (as in some areas of Asia) which creates the difficulties in providing schools and jobs for today's children and youth; rather it is the recent high *rates* of population growth against the background of rural under-development.

Nigeria, Ethiopia, and Zaïre are the three countries with more than 20 million inhabitants; another 25 nations have between 1 and 15 million; the remaining 7 have less than 1 million. The question has been raised whether some of these countries, with their limited internal markets, have sufficient population to generate a significant pace of industrial development. This consideration has given impetus to sub-regional groupings: functional associations for co-operation among adjoining nations in trade, transport, industrial location, and financial payments. This co-operation has been established in East Africa and is being encouraged in other areas by the Economic Commission for Africa.

More important than the low total populations of many of these nations is the uneven spread of peoples. A common characteristic is the large urban centre (or centres) with the rest of th population scattered thinly over the countryside, frequently wit considerable areas of economic backwardness. The attraction o these cities as key centres of administration and commerce ha been heightened in recent years by the location of new industries Available statistics show urban growth rates are often as high a 8 per cent or more each year; thus Dakar 7, Nairobi 7, Accra 8 Bamako 8, Abidjan 9, Dar es Salaam 9, and Lusaka 12. Wit this rapid population increase in the urban centres, government are strongly pressured to provide more schools as well as othe public amenities.

In many rural areas, on the other hand, the wide dispersal o peoples means weak common demand as well as high cost pe capita of investments in social and economic infrastructure (elec tric power, transport routes, water supply, education and healt services). Where widely-spread peoples can be gathered mor closely, the higher population density creates a situation of lowe cost and better service. These economies appear to justify i some areas the organized migration to new or enlarged rural sett lements.

These demographic elements – the size of the population, it variations in density, and its composition (with multiple ethni groups accounting for difficulties in national integration) – ob viously affect the expansion and the costs of education. The mos powerful single factor, however, behind the massive task o providing education and jobs for the present generation has bee the sharp rise in rates of population growth.

Throughout the 1950s the rates of population growth of thes African nations rose steadily until, in the mid-1960s, they level led off between 2 and 3 per cent net increase per annum, with a average of around 2.5 per cent. Accounting for these high rate of population increase has been the wider dissemination c health education and medical services with the consequent de cline in the death rate. Adults are living longer. Of greater importance, more children are surviving the precarious years of infancy.

The focus on the educational requirements for young people needs to be extended in time. What are the expected numbers of children who will be reaching school age at particular stages in the future: 5 years, 10 years, 20 years from now? The indications are clear enough. Where an annual increase of 2.5 is maintained, the population will double every 28 years: and the number of potential entrants to schools will also double. With an annual increase of 3 per cent the time interval is shortened to 23 years. It is therefore reasonable to consider education designs for the year 2000 based on populations double their present size and with cities five times as large as now.

Within the present context, what are the implications of these high rates of population growth?

– Between 40 and 50 per cent of total populations are below the age of 15 with consequent dependence on adult workers for provision for food, clothing, shelter, and health. In proportion to their populations, the nations of tropical Africa have twice as many young people under the age of 15 as do the countries of Western Europe and North America.

– Large families often mean poorly-fed children. Not only will these children lack physical fitness and stamina as they grow up, but recent studies have shown that inadequate nutrition in infancy contributes to lack of mental development.

– If expectations for improved living standards are to be met, then the rate of economic advancement will have to exceed the annual net increase in population by a significant margin. During the period since 1960 annual rates of economic growth have averaged around 4.5 per cent, but with populations increasing at the high rate of 2.5 per cent, the rise in income per person has been held down correspondingly. This economic performance compares well with rates of growth achieved by industrialized countries during the same period; however, population increase in these advanced countries was not much above 1 per cent and thus the proportionate increase in per capita income has been higher.

– In terms of education, such increases in numbers of children require many more schools and teachers and thus higher capital investments and recurrent costs – even to keep present proportions of school-age children in primary schools. Thus, the advance towards universal primary education becomes more formidable.

– Because of the increasing numbers of young entrants to the labour force each year, the problem of making the economic arrangements that would create suitable beginning employment opportunities for youth becomes more difficult.

Population policies, now being adopted by several nations, ultimately could have the effect of reducing the rate of increase. It is important to emphasise, however, that these policies are most suitably designed as part of a comprehensive strategy for social and economic development. The immediate problem concerns education and jobs for the children who have already been born.

3 Impediments of poor health and malnutrition

When governments intervene with public funds to help rural communities to prepare children for their life vocations, the attempts are usually to influence all stages of personal development: pre-school, school age, and post-school age. But funds are so small and the need so great. Priorities vary among countries in the emphasis accorded to health and nutrition, formal schooling, and out-of-school vocational training.

The presence of widespread malnutrition and multiple diseases not only affects children's chances for survival but also their potentialities for full mental and physical development. As a consequence their capacities for learning in the classroom and on the job are impaired. Under such unfavourable conditions, young people often grow into adulthood with chronic disabilities, lacking the vitality to change their environment. Poor health represents one of the most persistent factors explaining the continuity of rural poverty.

Mass immunization campaigns, together with the spread of medical facilities and para-medical services, are undoubtedly essential to the eradication of communicable diseases and the amelioration of illness. But education for better health also has an important place in the effort for rural improvement. Through such media as radio programmes in the vernacular languages, films shown by mobile units, well-designed posters, demonstrations and talks, adults in a rural community can be brought to an understanding of, for example, how guinea worms are transmitted and how children get *kwashiorkor,* the extreme form of protein deficiency. Particularly when related to local problems such as contaminated water supplies or lack of sanitation, these methods of education can lead to direct action and immediate results as well as to long-term benefits. In cases where whole villages suffer from lack of balanced diet, agricultural services have a part, too, in introducing the new crops which would add greater protein and other deficient nutrients. Villagers might themselves construct fishponds once they understand the design and have confidence that the basic stock of fish can be obtained. Here the agencies of community development help in motivating the enterprise for improved nutrition.

Through most parts of tropical Africa public expenditures on health improvement have been given low priority, not so much from neglect as from the pressures for resource use elsewhere. A familiar economic view has been that expenditures on health (including community health education) are oriented towards consumption rather than investment; therefore a minimum layout fosters human welfare but is not significant for higher economic growth. Economic growth, the argument goes, calls for a restraint on consumption and an increase in savings to enable investment in the main lines of development: agriculture, industry, power, transport. Increasingly, this view is being questioned. In fact, over a certain range of expenditures on health, productivity can be raised without any additional investment in complementary factors. Apart from its effect on economic output, increased expenditure on health affecting large numbers of rural people also means some reduction in the inequalities of income.

In the past, public expenditures on health and medicine have been heavily weighted in favour of urban as opposed to rural areas. Hospitals are almost always located in cities, consistent with their services to larger numbers of people and the demands of the educated *élites*. And thus, while there may be clusters of doctors, nurses, and medical facilities in the main cities, none at all may be available in the more remote areas where people are living at subsistence level. In recent years new ideas on resource allocation have stressed greater attention to low-cost paramedical services spread out over wide areas as a balance to the concentration of high-cost medical personnel and facilities in cities.

Emphasis is now being placed on the prevention of diseases rather than their cure, on the social group and the environment rather than the individual, on low-cost assistance for the many rather than high-cost care for the few. These promising ideas have yet to be applied widely in the vast rural areas.

A major difficulty in assessing rural needs for medical facilities and health education has been the lack of reliable information at local levels. For a few particular areas epidemiological studies have been made by research workers, usually attached to medical schools, and these are useful for assessing requirements in these areas as well as providing models for future surveys. Certainly the variety of ecological and cultural backgrounds present different health problems. In some areas, the suppression of malaria may be a priority, while in others the eradication of river flies which cause blindness to large numbers of children. Situations are familiar in which communities living at subsistence level have well-balanced diets including such high-protein foods as milk, meat, and fish; while other communities with relatively high incomes from cash crops have a high proportion of children with symptoms of *kwashiorkor*. Obviously, designs for community medicine and for health education must be based on local situations.

A recent report of the World Health Organization on nutrition has set out four conditions deserving highest priority.

– *Protein-calorie malnutrition,* primarily a problem of infants and children up to five years of age, is fatal in its severe forms and, in its more moderate cases, causes impaired growth and possibly mental retardation. This condition often begins before birth with maternal malnutrition causing a low birth-weight and it worsens after about the age of five months when the mother's breast-milk becomes inadequate and at the same time the infant suffers from diarrhoea and such other common diseases as measles, whooping cough, and respiratory infections. This condition develops, in fact, as a combination of malnutrition (deficiency of calories, proteins, and other essential nutrients) and infectious diseases. It has been estimated that of the children from birth to five years of age in developing countries, 3 per cent suffer from severe protein-calorie malnutrition and another 20 per cent from moderate malnutrition.

– *Xerophthalmia,* or *Vitamin A deficiency,* also mainly affects infants and young children. This condition prevails over wide areas, contributes to the mortality of undernourished children, and causes dramatic irreversible damage – blindness – in its extreme forms.

– *Iron-deficiency anemia* has a high prevalence among African children. In those up to age 15 the frequency of anemia varies between 30 and 60 per cent and even higher figures have been recorded for children under seven. Among adults 6 to 17 per cent of men and 15 to 50 per cent of women have been found iron-deficient, with a consequent lack of vitality.

– *Endemic goitre* occurs in people of all ages. While the most serious complications are found in adults, the pathological changes begin in childhood. Because iodine deficiency is the main causal factor, solutions to this condition can more easily be mounted on a mass scale – such as classical programmes of salt iodization or the more recent use of iodized oil.

This report concludes that while there has been a reduction in child mortality, there are no indications that nutrition for young children has improved much during the past 20 years. On the positive side, however, gains have been made in the virtual eradication of such deficiency diseases as scurvy, pellagra, and beri-beri and in the increasing control over some communicable diseases which help to precipitate severe malnutrition, such as malaria and measles. A number of the nations of tropical Africa have established nutrition units within the ministries of health or agriculture. A few nations have set up nutrition rehabilitation centres. And in general, there is much greater awareness at high political levels of the seriousness of the situation.

At the national level, education for better health belongs as an essential part of the programmes of ministries of health in controlling communicable diseases and in improving nutrition on a wide scale. It also comes into the broader scope of rural transformation, integrated with programmes of agriculture and community development, in the effort to raise incomes and heighten standards of living.

At its most intimate level, health education is family-centred. A child is born into a family setting, cared for by its mother, father, perhaps a grandmother, and older brothers and sisters. If the mother has an understanding of the suitable foods to supplement breast milk for the growing baby and if a clinic is near at hand for immunization and advice on infant illnesses, then the child is likely to get a strong start in life. In many cases, however, the mother herself is under-nourished and overburdened with the duties of carrying water and fuel, pounding cereals and tubers, cultivating and weeding, carrying loads long distances to markets. Clearly the nutrition and general vitality of the mother is closely associated with the health of her children. Health education will only have effective results when family living conditions are improved.

Family planning measures are also part of this picture. When rural people perceive that their children will survive and grow up into healthy adults, they will be more likely to limit the numbers. And in turn, the smaller families will mean greater quality of care and education for children. Only four African countries have explicit programmes of family planning; more have implicit ones. But however vigorously these programmes are introduced, they are not likeley to take effect in rural areas until parents are confident that children will survive to provide security for their old age.

Health education in schools gives young people the theories of how diseases are caused and the importance of personal hygiene, clean water supplies, community sanitation, and balanced diets. These lessons lay the foundations for improvement for the next generation. They are not likely to change present village life, however, unless adults also understand the issues and have the opportunities to take action. Here is an example of how education in school becomes more effective when related to out-of-school learning and with other programmes of community development.

Learning activities outside and inside classrooms

4 Indigenous learning processes

It is a truism that as they grow up all children receive out-of-school education. They learn from their parents and other relatives, from older brothers and sisters, from ritual and recreational activities within the community. They learn the language, the oral literature, and the religious teachings of their family group (often influenced through such institutions as church or mosque). They learn social values and accepted ways of behaving. And it is out of school that many rural young people, the great majority, gain the vocational training for their life work.

How does a child who does not attend school (or who goes for only a year or so) learn the basis for his life occupation and become absorbed into the labour force? Girls learn their future roles and duties by gradually doing the jobs assigned to women: caring for younger children, preparing vegetables and pounding yams, carrying water. At the same time, boys progressively take on the work of men by herding cattle, repairing houses and granaries, helping to plant and to harvest crops. For many children, in fact, the transition from helping with duties inside the family and beginning to work purposefully is imperceptible. The characteristic form of enterprise in any rural area in tropical Africa is the self-employed family unit: the farm or cattle herd, the craft or artisan workshop, the stall in the market, the small transport business. Children who do not go to school often become 'economically active' at about age seven and learn on the job. Some children in a family may learn the occupations of their parents; others may be apprenticed to relatives to diversify their training. Here are some typical examples.

A boy from a farming family has no opportunity for formal schooling. At about the age when others start to school, he begins his training by accompanying his father to the family farm plots. At first his duties may not be very difficult; he carries tools, assists where he can with the hoeing and harvesting, helps to bring back some of the farm products to the family home. Gradually, as he grows stronger, he becomes more able to perform the seasonal operations involved in farming. In many societies by the time he is ready for marriage, he is prepared to start farming on his own.

Another boy, whose father is also a farmer, may be apprenticed to a relative who is a master carpenter. In the beginning he will help to keep the workshop neat, learn to use the saw and the hammer and to measure correctly, and in the slack seasons he may help on his master's farm. After perhaps five years, he will become a journeyman; and later he will become a master carpenter and take in his own apprentices.

Or a young girl becomes apprenticed to a relative who is a woman trader in textiles. At first she may only sweep the premises and run errands; gradually she learns to make correct money transactions; finally she is trusted to go out herself with lengths of cloth to sell. After some years of work experience and the accumulation of modest savings, she will begin trading on her own.

The quality and types of indigenous vocational training for young people vary by family and community, by culture, by economic circumstance. Besides the domestic skills for running the household, this out-of-school education includes a wide range of arts and crafts – from the traditional ones of weaving and wood carving to contemporary ones of machine sewing and vehicle repairing. Young people are spending long hours in village markets, in workshops, on building sites. They are acquiring the techniques of working with wood (carvers, carpenters), metal (blacksmiths, goldsmiths), leather (tanners, shoe and sandal makers), cloth (weavers, tailors, seamstresses), with raffia and cane (hat, chair, and mat makers).

From these learning processes within families has arisen a system of apprenticing – more evident in some rural areas of tropical Africa than in others – expressed through written or verbal understandings. This is, in effect, a procedure for learning a variety of skills on the job within modest small-scale enterprises. The distinction is sometimes made that these indigenous learning procedures are static, passing on only traditional skills, while modern schooling alone provides the dynamic necessary to transform societies. Such a contrast is misleading, particularly when it can be demonstrated that new skills are being infused through this indigenous learning system. Here the rural-urban interaction has a strong effect. For example, a young man from a farming family has the opportunity to serve as an apprentice in the city t a relative who repairs various motor vehicles. After about fiv years of apprenticeship and perhaps a few more in a paid posi tion, this young adult has been able to gather the necessary too and he now goes back to his home area to set up business on main road. And, in turn, he takes on apprentices. Large number of competent farmers, artisans, and traders (men and women some who have never been to school, have progressed by learn ing on the job and by using intelligent initiatives.

While it is important to emphasize the *positive* elements withi indigenous learning processes in rural communities, it is equall important to note their *shortcomings*. Obviously, parents an other adults cannot teach skills to young people that they do nc themselves possess. It follows that any assistance to raise th technical performances of adults – through extension services c governments, by voluntary organizations – will eventually hel these young learners. Assistance, for example, provided throug agricultural extension services on how to grow new varieties c crops, how to prevent infestation of disease in animals and seed lings, how to improve cattle herds, enables adults to pass o these new practices.

The traditional learning processes, which occur mainly withi families and local communities, are themselves changing with th societies which generate them. These learning processes are ex tended, modified, or transformed by varied influences. Centra among these is the changing economy: market incentives, im provements in economic infrastructure, and the supplementar education provided through programmes of extension services c governments and through specific projects. Unquestionabl another important influence is the school.

5 The spread of formal schooling

Among the nations of tropical Africa during the 1960s, wide spread primary schooling was accorded a pivotal role in develop ment. This was early affirmed at the 1961 Addis Ababa confe ence of ministers of education when the goal was set for universal primary education by 1980. Strenuous efforts were made throughout the decade in expanding school facilities. By 1970 several countries had managed to double their enrolments; others were still far from their targets.

This determination to provide primary education for all African children was explained by the following reasons:

– Education, including literacy in the national language, is a basic human right.

– Without strong efforts to expand formal education the great proportion of the next generation would be illiterate, a situation inconsistent with development needs.

– Widespread basic education would yield high social and economic outcomes, including greater participation in national and local discussions on development and greater capacities for accepting innovations; these outcomes would warrant the high financial outlays.

– A sufficiently wide base of primary education must exist in order to make acceptable selections for the secondary level.

The Addis Ababa conference in 1961 was remarkable both for the targets set and for the detailed explorations on how to reach these objectives. The training of teachers at various levels, salaries of teachers, the supply and equipment of classrooms, the production and distribution of suitable textbooks: all these components were considered.

Targets established for 1980 were: that primary education would be universal, free, and compulsory; 30 per cent of the relevant age group would be receiving second-level education; and 20 per cent of those completing second-level education would find places in higher-level education. Interim targets for 1970 wer set at 70 per cent of school-age children in primary schools, 1 per cent at the second level.

Despite dedicated efforts, by 1970, of the 40 million primar school-age children, the proportions reached were only 38 pe cent (15.2 million) enrolled in primary schools and 7 per cent (million) of the age-group attending second-level education. Th proportions achieved thus amounted to roughly half those set fo the interim target. A point to note is that secondary school enrol ments increased at a faster rate than primary. The average of th national rates of increase of enrolments during the 1960s were per cent each year at primary and 14 per cent each year a secondary level.

On the negative side, the 1970 figures reveal that some 62 pe cent (24.8 million) of school-age children were not attendin primary schools. If the rural areas were taken separately, thi proportion would be closer to 70 per cent.

These overall proportions of primary school enrolments, how ever, conceal a variety of national achievements. Individua countries are grouped here according to their enrolment percen tages in 1970.

In the *first group* are seven countries with enrolments between and 21 per cent. Included are five French-speaking West Africa countries and two others.

Somalia	8
Upper Volta	10
Mauritania	12
Niger	12
Ethiopia	13
Mali	19
Chad	21

The *second group* has 11 countries with enrolments between 24 and 33 per cent.

Burundi	24
Gambia	25
Guinca	26
Tanzania	29
Liberia	30
Sierra Leone	30
Dahomey	31
Malawi	31
Uganda	31
Nigeria	32
Senegal	33

In the *third group* are 14 countries with enrolments between 49 and 71 per cent. This includes nine central and southern African countries, three of the west coast of the continent, and two others – Kenya and Madagascar.

Ivory Coast	49
Togo	52
Kenya	54
Swaziland	54
Madagascar	55
Rwanda	55
Botswana	56
Central African Republic	57
Ghana	61
Zaïre	61
Lesotho	65
Cameroons	68
Equatorial Guinea	68
Zambia	71

The fourth group has three countries with enrolment ratios between 87 and 93 per cent.

Congo (Peoples' Republic)	87
Gabon	91
Mauritius	93

The following generalizations are relevant to the present context

– Countries with the *very lowest* proportions of primary school-age children in school have a number of characteristics in common. They are mainly arid or semi-arid. They have small populations (except for Ethiopia) and low population density (around four inhabitants per square kilometre). They have large numbers of nomadic people as well as areas of widely-dispersed villages. They have low levels of urban development with an average of five per cent of the population living in towns of more than 20,000 inhabitants. Finally, of those attending schools, girls make up a low percentage.

– Countries with the *very highest* proportions of school-age children in schools have small populations: together comprising about one per cent of the total population of the 35 countries. They have a high degree of urbanization. Also, in these countries the numbers of girls more closely approximate the numbers of boys attending schools.

– For 29 of the 35 countries the expansion of school enrolments slowed down between 1965 and 1970 as compared with the period 1960 to 1965. The other six countries, however, had a more rapid increase and this accounts for about half the increase in total enrolments of the 35 countries during 1965 to 1970.

– Starting ages for primary schools vary. In 19 countries the starting age is six, the remainder at age 7. The number of pupils to one teacher range from 14 to 50 and beyond.

inging home firewood

8
Boys learn on the farm
after school hours

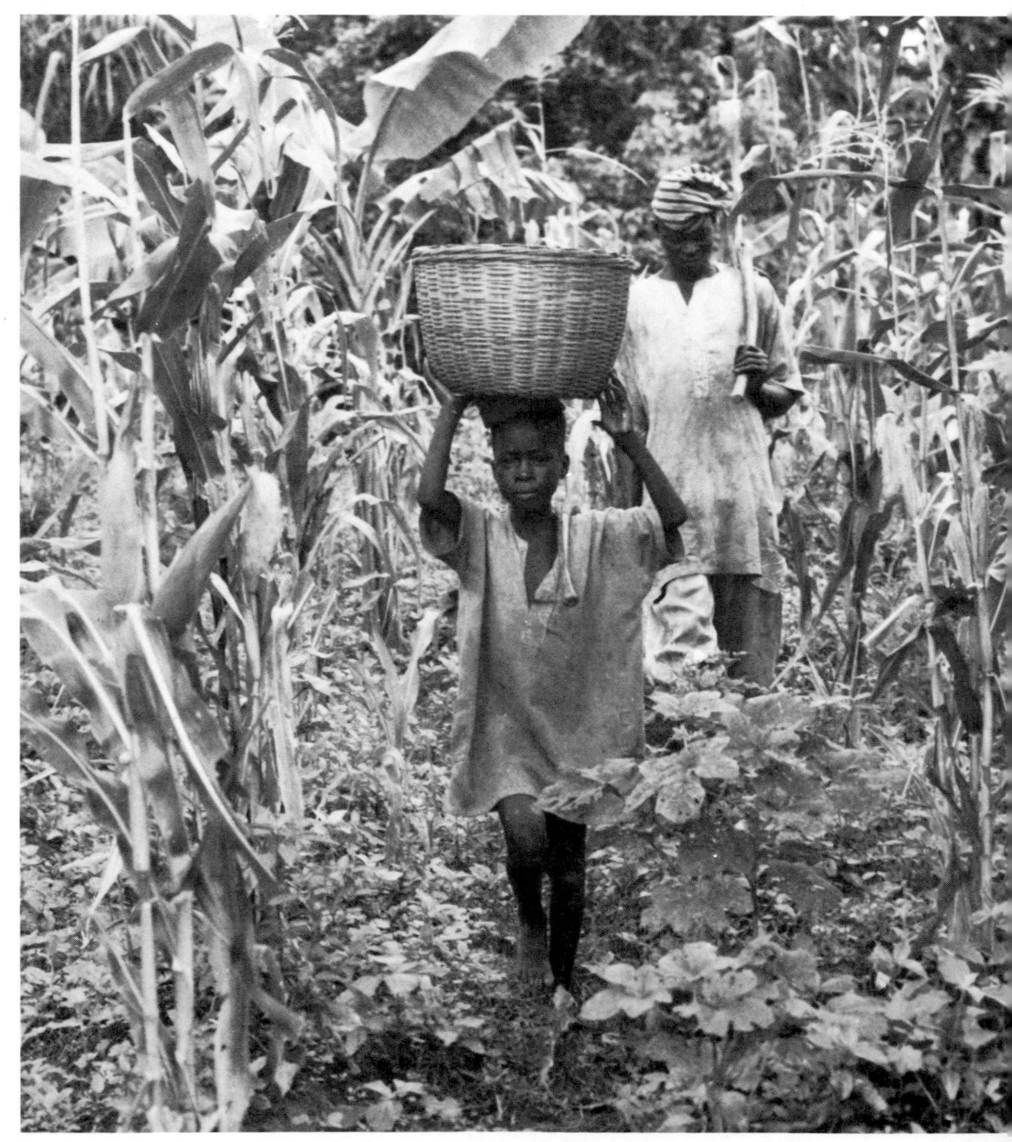

– In primary schools the overall ratio is about two girls for every three boys, but in secondary schools the division widens with approximately two girls for every five boys.

– Koranic schools, some with specific buildings to meet in, some without, are significant in a number of countries, especially those bordering the Sahara. Their numbers are difficult to estimate, and so too their importance for development.

In the process of expanding primary education a number of difficulties were revealed, economic and educational, which differed in severity from one country to another. Certain problems, however, are general.

inance

Foremost among these difficulties has been the strain on central and local governments' budgets in paying for primary schooling, particularly recurrent costs, with teachers' salaries and teachers' training absorbing over three-quarters of the payments. Differences exist among national economies in the emphasis on expansion of primary relative to secondary, post-primary vocational classes, polytechnic institutions, and universities. Typically, expenditures for recurrent costs of formal education rose to absorb from 20 to 25 per cent of total public expenditures, over half of which was used for primary schooling. In general, very low proportions of budgets were allocated to out-of-school education such as literacy classes and education through extension services for health, agriculture, and community development.

ropouts

In the estimates at the Addis Ababa Conference provision was made for a yearly attrition from primary school classes, but the actual dropouts far exceeded the number forecast. A typical situation in several countries: of 100 pupils who started in primary grade one, one-half had given up by grade four, perhaps one-third attained the final grade and an even lesser percentage completed the full primary course. Frequently this meant a reduction in the size of classes taught by one teacher and thus a significant rise in the recurrent unit cost per pupi Reasons for the high rate of dropouts were varied: inability c families to meet school fees or, in areas where no fees wei charged, to meet such modest expenses as school uniforms; th labour contribution of older children was required at home or o the family farm; a recognition by parents that there was less like lihood than in former years that schooling would lead to bette paying jobs than those available within the family enterprise.

Falling quality

With the hurried expansion of primary schooling unqualifie teachers were hired when qualified ones were not availabl (particularly in rural areas), textbooks and equipment were ofte in short supply, school buildings sometimes were not ready at th appointed time, administrative officers at all levels were unde pressure. These reasons have been given for the reduction i quality of education noted by civil servants, educators, and com mission reports in various countries.

Inequalities in distribution of facilities

Evident particularly in the lesser numbers of schools relative t populations in rural areas. The effect of low population densi for establishing and running schools is almost uniformly nega tive. A school can only serve a limited area, usually up to a five mile radius, and therefore is less likely to gain economies of scal from the optimum number of pupils. Added to these higher un costs per pupil are the expenses of boarding facilities and tran port services offered in some countries. Again, because of lon distances children are found to be absent from school more day of the year. In sparsely-populated areas construction costs fc buildings are almost invariably higher. Qualified teachers a often difficult to recruit and to keep.

What is not so clear, however, is whether the fact of the propo tionately few schools in particular rural communities might b explained as a supply problem (inability or unwillingness c governments to provide facilities) or a demand problem (lack c interest among local parents for primary schooling).

Relevance of the curriculum

This is the most vigorously debated of all topics relating to the development of education in Africa today. The arguments are complex with varied degrees of emphasis, but divide into two main lines. One side advocates considering the curriculum terminal for those (around 85 to 90 per cent) who cannot go on to secondary schools and thus making it much more job-centred, practical, and geared to local economic activities. The other side argues that the purpose of primary schools is not to teach young boys and girls occupational skills but to teach them literacy and numeracy; that the establishment of such vocational primary schools would create a tier of schools recognized by parents as inferior to the more academic ones.

Employment problem of school leavers

In many nations primary school leavers have increasing difficulties in finding beginning work that represents any improvement over what they might have done with no schooling at all. This is a harsh commentary on the slow pace of development, particularly in rural areas.

One conclusion that follows from this summary of education expansion is that a number of countries will have to postpone the date for achieving universal primary schooling until perhaps one or two or more decades beyond 1980. A few nations have already revised their objectives and plan to hold, for the time being, the proportion of children gaining primary education to a defined percentage. Tanzania, for example, aims to build up and maintain its primary school attendance at 50 per cent of school-age population. This percentage is considered as providing a sufficient basis for the selection of entrants to secondary and technical education while at the same time not being excessive in relation to demands on public funds for the development of other aspects of the economy.

6 School leavers and their quest for jobs

In most of the countries of tropical Africa, out of every 1,00 who reach a standard of permanent literacy in primary school only 10 to 15 per cent go on to secondary schooling; thus at th end of the primary stage 850 to 900 are ready to start work Those who come from farming families often reject the occupa tions of their parents. They feel (and their families usually sup port them) that their schooling has fitted them for tasks wit better prospects. Many boys after they reach the age of 15 or s migrate to stay with relatives in towns and cities and hope the will get wage-paid jobs. They are now able to read and write i the national language, to deal with numbers of reasonable com plexity, but they have no particular vocational skills to offer a employer. Many of them hope to find an attachment which give them training on the job and develops their potential skills. Bu very few jobs are available and competition is intense.

Basic to the employment problem of school leavers are tw elements: the sharp rise in rates of population increase and th rapid expansion of schooling facilities. Against this general back ground are the many variables of rural life: the availability c land and other natural resources, the characteristics of econc mies and their pace of development, the cultural settings.

In areas where land surface is restricted, the larger families mak it necessary with the existing technology of hoe and blade, tha fallow periods be shortened; then, without added fertilizers, th fertility of the soil deteriorates. Where money incomes fror farming are very low or non-existent, not only must the produc of the farm be shared among greater numbers but there are fe or no opportunities off the farm. With increasing numbers c children attending the local schools, it is only natural tha parents will encourage their educated sons to go to relatives i the city and search for work.

Even in areas where there are cash crops, the increasing number of young adults require that some of a group of sons must fin places off the family farm, whether in farming elsewhere, in local non-farming jobs, or in the city. It is usually the unschooled and those with only a few years of primary schooling who stay on the family land; while the more senior school leavers try for a job in the city at least for a trial period.

This migration often depends on patterns already existing and the continuity of ethnic associations between rural and urban areas. In earlier decades school leavers coming to the cities found jobs and worked their way up in these organizations; they then provided a base for others from their home area while the newcomers, in turn, looked for work. The difference now is that many more school leavers, including those raised in urban areas, are competing for the few jobs.

In the cities of tropical Africa the educated young account for half to three-quarters, at least, of those openly unemployed. While the problem is widely recognized, statistical assessments of the extent of unemployment among school leavers (and, even more, of the under-utilization of human resources generally) are difficult to achieve. Quoted statistics normally refer only to the openly unemployed in urban areas. They do not thus reveal the difficulties of (a) those who are employed part-time, usually as a means of helping to pay for personal living costs, while they seek work with better returns, (b) those fully employed but below their present capabilities and with little chance for developing their talents later, (c) those insecurely employed, and (d) young women who have attended schools and are without jobs and yet are not recorded as unemployed unless they have specific qualifications such as teachers, nurses, secretaries.

For policy purposes, it is important that each nation should know more about the numbers and the characteristics of these job-seeking young people: ages and education, positions in families, background and living conditions, migratory movements, aspirations, periods unemployed. The incidence of unemployment in different parts of the country should also b charted.

Although the evidence is fragmentary and not immediately com parable among countries, the following examples provide indica tions of the problem. Of the approximate half-million opcnly un employed in the cities of Nigeria in 1966, over three-quarter were between the ages of 15 and 25, with a median age of 19 almost all of these young people were male school leavers. A official report from Kenya in 1967 states that of 150,00 primary school leavers, 22 per cent went on to secondar schools, 1 per cent to post-primary classroom vocational train ing, 15 per cent obtained some employment, while at the time c the enquiry a high proportion of the remaining 62 per cent wer looking for jobs; since 1967, unemployed secondary schoc leavers have taken over as prior urgency for government actior Sample surveys in 1968 in Douala and Yaounde, Cameroons indicate rates of unemployment of 13 and 17 per cent respective ly; in Abidjan, Ivory Coast, the estimate in 1963 was 20 pe cent. For Mauritius, the 1967 Report on the Economy states tha with employment showing little expansion, there was a substan tial increase in the numbers of unemployed, among whom wer large numbers of both primary and secondary school leavers.

How do the employment difficulties of these school leavers diffe from those who never went to school at all? Those without for mal education usually take up the work of their parents o relatives and learn on the job from an early age. Their possibili ties for choice are limited; they are more likely to follow th customary occupations of their home area. School leavers, on th other hand, have often acquired heightened expectations as result of their formal education. The economic environmen however, does not generate the required jobs in sufficient quan tities to fulfil these aspirations.

While in most of these countries primary school leavers an

dropouts from the early years of secondary schools make up the great bulk of the unemployed, increasingly secondary school graduates are noted as part of the problem. Familiar for some years in parts of Asia, this situation is now becoming more evident in Africa: for example, in Mauritius, Nigeria, Kenya.

During this past decade the employment problem of school leavers has become of central concern to governments. From the viewpoint of parents, the reward for sending children to school is that educated youth should gain higher money returns and therefore be in a better position to help younger children and, eventually, their parents in old age. At government level, those responsible for economic policy have recognized the major imbalance between the expanding systems of formal education and the slow pace of rural economic development.

This widespread unemployment is considered of critical importance because the numbers are large, continuing to increase, and the problem is not correcting itself. Such unemployment has a high social and economic cost. Not only does it represent personal misery for each family, but also a waste of human resources on a national scale, involving a delayed return on the high investment in education from scarce public resources.

A large exodus of educated youth from the rural areas could delay agricultural modernization or even retard present agricultural production. At the same time, too rapid an influx into cities strains the capacity of municipal facilities: of water supplies, sanitation, transport, health services, housing. Hence the shanty habitations in many African cities today.

Since the distribution of income and property is unequal in most of these nations, unemployment of this magnitude accentuates these inequalities by pressing down the earnings of the self-employed. If the society becomes more and more divided into those who enjoy the conspicuous comforts of modern living and those who are excluded, large numbers of youthful unemployed present a distinct threat to national stability. Emergency measures may then be considered necessary which might well be in contradiction to the main designs of national economic development.

7 Obstacles to raising incomes of rural producers

Improvements in education alone cannot solve the employment problem of rural school leavers. This is self-evident. Yet discussions continue as if educational adjustments (changing the primary curriculum, providing more post-primary vocational courses, introducing new types of out-of-school learning) would *by themselves* alleviate unemployment. So long as these school leavers see around them an environment that is technologically static, where money incomes are low, excessive numbers will continue to migrate to the towns and cities. And so long as the money wages of clerks and messengers in city offices are several times higher than the money incomes from their family farms school leavers will continue to try and get these wage-paid jobs. Understandably, some persist and remain for long periods without work. First and foremost, the solutions to the employment problem are economic. More opportunities for renumerative work are required in the rural areas.

Providing more opportunities for rural youth is only one component, however, of the problem of raising the economic status of all unemployed and underemployed: youth and adults, male and female, the educated and those without formal schooling, in both rural and urban areas. The employment difficulty of rural youth thus brings to attention the widespread underemployment characterized by extremely low economic productivity of much of the labour force – for example, in farming, petty trading, small workshops. At present, perhaps 20 to 25 per cent of the labour forces of most nations of tropical Africa could be considered as being under-utilized. *For the 1970s no economic issue is more critical than this: getting more people involved in more productive work with consequent higher money returns.*

Such generation of widespread productive employment in any particular nation depends on the pace and characteristics of its overall economic progress. In the factors determining this, the 35 nations of tropical Africa reveal considerable diversity: in demographic features, natural resources, socio-economic and political circumstances.

For all countries, exports are the chief dynamic for economic growth. Several countries have mineral resources (Nigeria and Gabon, oil; Zambia and Zaïre, copper), but for most of the nations the principal exports are agricultural products. Export prices, however, have a history of instability and, accordingly, government revenues and plans for economic development can be seriously distorted. A few countries regularly generate from their current budgets sufficient surpluses for substantial capital projects; but for many nations government savings are often negative, with consequent heavy annual payments for foreign debt. In addition, tropical African countries include 13 of the world's 18 landlocked low-income countries, whose unfavourable transport tariffs and port facilities have the effect of retarding their trade expansion.

The nations with high populations, and thus with large internal markets, have an obvious advantage in getting going a process of industrialization while those with around a million or less have little possibility of industrial growth except through economic association with neighbouring countries.

Also, countries differ in their strategies for economic development. Nigeria, for example, is evolving a 'mixed economy' of public and private enterprise. Tanzania, on the other hand, is acting on its conviction that the only acceptable method of reducing pronounced imbalances in income distribution is through socialized production methods. This approach is exemplified in the policy of gathering scattered farm families into *ujamaa* ('working together') villages throughout the countryside.

These nations have their own values and religions which also contribute towards their styles of development. Over thirty of the countries became independent in a space of 15 years (prominent exceptions being Ethiopia and Liberia, which already had their separate identities). Because of past foreign domination, French or English remain as official languages and patterns of international trade reflect the former colonial associations. Each country has a variety of ethnic groups, speaking different languages, which sometimes makes national political cohesion difficult. The strength of association within extended families with their networks of reciprocal relationships, varies according to cultures. Such loyalties may have the effect of reducing the level of economic savings and capital formation but also of providing an important measure of social security.

An indication of the level of economic development is revealed by the following international comparisons. The total gross domestic product of the 35 nations is less than that of Benelux (Belgium, Netherlands, Luxembourg); of the 14 nations of West Africa, less than that of Turkey; of the 8 countries of Central Africa, less than that of Peru; of the 13 countries of East Africa less than that of Finland and about equal to Norway.

Measured by annual rates of increase in gross national product the economic performances range widely but compare well with those for other developing countries. And any review of the 1960s should include the encouraging indices of improvements in physical infrastructure, expansion of education and health services, and the creation of minimum administrative services. Even so, 16 of the 25 countries defined by UNCTAD (United Nations Conference on Trade and Development) in 1971 as the world's poorest, where gross domestic product per year is less than $ 100 per person, are in tropical Africa.

Generating significantly more jobs in the rural economy – and creating a milieu in which further meaningful employment can be self-created – depends on measures taken throughout the economy. At present, certain elements negative to employment creation are found in the development patterns of most tropical African nations.

The high capital intensity of most new investment

Labour absorption of major modern and semi-modern establishments is limited: in the public service, large industries, the principal commercial and transport enterprises. While headway has been made in setting up new industries, the number of workers employed by these enterprises in most countries is still quite low. Large industry is capital-intensive and does not account for the employment of more than 5 to 8 per cent of the labour forces.

Further investigations are required to determine where the margins of advantage really are as between labour-intensity and capital-intensity in promoting development. For some establishments (for example, large industrial firms, major public works) the economic advantage may prove to be with the use of large units of plant, equipment, and specialized organization, requiring few employees compared with capital invested.

Where large amounts of labour can be used economically is in farming, small-scale industries, and in minor public works. Greater intimacy with the aptitudes and the modest accomplishments of peasant farmers, craftsmen and small-scale entrepreneurs will undoubtedly reveal a wide range of possibilities for creating higher incomes at no great expense in public funds. Labour intensity and rising output may turn out to be more harmonious than is commonly supposed.

The rural-urban imbalance in average incomes, location of industries, and investment in amenities

This polarity does not mean that all family incomes in cities are uniformly high while those in villages are all extremely low but that the wage-earners in cities usually gain substantially higher rewards than the self-employed, the large majority, in rural areas. Trade-union strength often contributes to the upward pressure of money wage rates in the cities greatly out of proportion to rates of return on farms and in other rural family enterprises. (Such an upward move in wages also encourages firms to substitute capital for labour, thus eliminating jobs that would otherwise be available.)

New industries are almost invariably clustered in the cities. The more jobs created through new urban-based industries, the greater is the movement to the cities of educated youth to compete for these opportunities. And the higher the numbers of openly unemployed. Cities also tend to be favoured in the distribution of amenities, such as transport systems, water supplies, cinemas, and libraries.

Transforming the rural areas will need to take higher priority if headway is to be made in creating more employment for young people. When farm families earn greater returns, the higher money circulation in villages creates more jobs off the farm: in trading, transport, building. Small-scale industries (processing farm products or working with wood, metal, cloth, leather) have more scope to meet consumer demand. And of considerable importance: new major industries need to be set up in rural towns or in newly-created rural industrial centres. In its present five-year plan, for example, Tanzania intends that almost all of the new industries will be located in rural towns.

Prices that misrepresent national objectives

Relative incomes for work are often extreme in the differences between the lowest and highest, and they are unrelated to national requirements for labour. The situation is familiar in which primary, secondary (including technical institutes) and university graduates receive beginning incomes in the ratio of 100, 250, and 900. In many instances, the incomes pegged for different levels and types of education between the public and private sectors, or within either of them, are inconsistent. When the step down to the next level is considerable, young people understandably will hold out to get the higher return and in the meantime remain unemployed.

Revaluations of salaries and wages would show ways of clearing these distortions and setting rewards more in line with national development objectives and employment requirements.

Barriers to the mobility of labour

Political, ethnic, and religious obstacles to the free movement of people often result in youth with surplus skills in one area being unable to move freely to another area where there is a deficit of such skills. Instances occur, for example, where in one area an apparent excess of secondary school leavers remain unemployed while in another such skills are needed in school teaching or within government, industrial, or commercial services. Clearly, policies that remove impediments to the free movement of qualified labour are important in helping to solve problems of unemployment.

The provision of employment is not considered a central objective of development

Until recently, strategies for development in tropical Africa have not given much attention to labour utilization. The usual argument is that rapid economic growth in output of goods and services should be the main objective and that income redistribution and increased employment can be achieved later through fiscal changes. In other words, if the economy is growing through the use of advanced technologies requiring relatively few workers, in time the benefits will filter down to everyone. Suppose that economic growth during the 1970s were to be achieved at 6 per cent per year, would this guarantee a significant advance in the quality of life for the majority of people? The answer is likely no. An increase in national incomes and outputs will not help the poor half of the population unless policies deliberately involve these families within the national economic effort.

In any case, and as a last resort, one per cent less in the growth of national economic output (resulting from the spreading of available capital more widely and involving even further jobs in the immediate future) may prove a small price to pay for social stability in the short term and, indeed, a vital advantage to society in the long term.

8 Educating adults for rural change

Whatever the procedures chosen in helping to raise the work performances and money returns of rural producers and to widen the range of amenities for rural families – through price adjustments, introducing more suitable and low-cost tools, building roads and clinics – education of adult men and women is a leading component. Much of this education occurs through the extension activities of departments of government: of agriculture, forestry, and fishing; health; education; community development; public works. And increasingly these days attempts are being made to support rural economic programmes by radio broadcasts in national and local languages and by functional literacy instruction.

Educating adult men and women in ways which improve their economic results provides an indirect means of educating young people who work with them. There are, thus, two procedures for bringing improved out-of-school learning to large numbers of rural young people. The *indirect method* concentrates on changing attitudes, including better occupational skills, and bringing practical knowledge to adults – who then pass on this learning to the next generation. The *direct approach* reaches young people themselves through young farmers' clubs, training, settlement projects, literacy classes, and so on.

Because of the severe limitation of funds and qualified personnel to teach through extension and other channels, decisions in the use of resources have to be of a closely-calculated 'more-or-less' type. On what age-group should presently-available, limited funds be spent? What should be the 'mix' of education as between adults and the young? One argument is that more should be spent on vocational and on-the-job training of adults, that this would lead to more immediate economic returns than, for instance, further investment in primary schooling, or more out-of-school education provided directly to young people. And that it is the present that matters most. Clearly, there are no set rules. Each nation will launch programmes and specific projects in volving adults and young people, as meets the situation being confronted.

Nevertheless, it is important to emphasize that *the majority of useful learning situations for rural young people come into being as a by-product of economic development.* This maxim applies to the most prevalent types of out-of-school education: the preparation of young people for their occupational roles and, later, on-the-job vocational education. An essential step, therefore, in creating more and better out-of-school learning activities for rural young people is through implementing policies for far-reaching rural development. And this involves helping the resource-managers of the tens of thousands of small-scale economic units throughout the countryside, farms and off-farm enterprises. In large part, this means helping adults.

Educating rural men and women requires altering their views about their own capabilities. Such education to change attitudes and, correspondingly, to inspire motivation, has been expressed by President Julius Nyerere of Tanzania, in a broadcast to his people entitled 'Adult Education Year 1970 in Prospect', as follows.

> We talk a lot about educating adults, quite a lot of people have been working in this field, but we have never really organized ourselves to attack Ignorance. The importance of adult education, both for our country and for every individual cannot be over-emphasised. We are poor, and backward; and too many of us just accept our present conditions as the 'will of God', and imagine that we can do nothing about them. In many cases, therefore, the first objective of adult education must be to shake ourselves out of a resignation to the kind of life Tanzanian people have lived for centuries past. We must become aware of the things we, as members of the human race, can do for ourselves and our country. We must learn to realise that we do not have to live miserably in hovels, or cultivate with bad *jembes*[1], or suffer from many diseases; we must learn that we ourselves can change these things. The first job of adult education will be to make us reject bad houses, bad *jembes,* and preventable diseases . . . It will make us recognize that we ourselves have the ability to obtain better houses, better tools and better health.

mbe, a digging hoe.

But what is adult education? Quite simply, it is learning about anythin at all which can help us to understand the environment we live in, an the manner in which we can change and use this environment in order t improve ourselves. Education is not just something that happens in class rooms. It is learning from others, and from our own experience of pas successes and failures. Education is learning from books, from the radic from films, from discussions about matters which affect our lives, an especially from doing things. This question of learning by doing is ver important.

The best way to learn to sew is to sew; the best way to learn to farm is t cultivate; the best way to learn cooking is to cook; the best way to lear how to teach is to teach; and so on. A child learns to walk by walking not by reading a book on how to walk. We learn from the experience c doing.

A natural question to ask is this: how do farming families lear new methods? They emulate neighbours who have adopted new variety of seedling or a new procedure in marketing. A social meetings or in local markets, they find out who has goo yields of high-quality crops and what led to this result. They ma travel to another area where they see more advanced, mor profitable ways of doing certain operations. Through the aggres sive salesmanship of a commercial firm, they may learn abou the value of fertilisers or insecticides. They listen to radio talk (through transistor sets, now widely available and shared, o through diffusion in the village) put on by agricultural extensio in local languages. They may observe government demonstratio plots and take part in classes which explain the new technique involved. Like practical people anywhere, they don't usuall bother about new ideas unless they can see some definite pay off: a higher money income, better living conditions, a mor appetising diet, or less back-breaking work to gain the sam results.

Yet, whether rural people take up new ideas quickly or slowl depends on their particular backgrounds. Among the nations c tropical Africa there is great variety in social and economic cor ditions. Even within one nation there may be many enviror

ɔung men at a farm
stitute working in
vegetable field

10
Learning to use
a tractor at
a farm institute

ments. Different natural resources mean contrasts in degrees of wealth and poverty; some areas have cash crops, plentiful land, or mineral wealth; while others have only subsistence farming and perhaps a shortage of fertile land. Different groups of rural people vary in their traditions, their ways of living, their initiatives, and their responses to existing, and new, market incentives and technical help.

For education of any kind (whether provided inside or outside classrooms) to yield its full benefits in changing the lives of rural people, the education must be closely allied to these local realities. Factors other than education almost certainly will need to be infused at the same time. For example, agricultural extension services (essentially a form of adult education) can only raise output of a suitable range of crops by providing complementary elements according to local needs: practical credit programmes, subsidized seedlings and insecticides, improved storage facilities, perhaps a tractor pool.

The resulting higher farm incomes mean higher money circulation locally and higher demand for goods and services. Some of these wants will likely be satisfied by imports or by the products of large factories in the cities. But the greater demand will also stimulate local small-scale production of goods and services — in tailoring, furniture-making, bicycle and motor truck repair services, minor construction works, and so on. And thus, in turn, more opportunities are created for young people for on-the-job training as apprentices. These youth may be school leavers from the village school as well as some who have not attended school at all.

The result of governments' help in raising productivity of farmers, by introducing simple innovations, will be more employment-creating (off the farm) than employment-displacing (on the farm). The opportunities for employment are modest. Whether these will occur in a particular area depends on the craft traditions of manual dexterity and on local initiative. But whether in the local area or at a distance, the existence of more off-farm involvement means more (and frequently better) out-of-school learning as apprentices.

Because of local variations in cultural, ecological, and economic circumstances, the approaches through education, of many kinds, including and in particular the field services of departments of government, vary according to local requirements.

Obviously, government extension services, at their best, are distributed lightly and concentrate on helping communities – not individual families (except when helping several 'master farmers' as demonstrators). Nevertheless, an example of one farming family brings out the needs and possibilities.

Take, for instance, a farm of around three to five acres, using simple tools such as the hoe and cutlass, practising bush fallowing by which cropped land is left fallow to recuperate over a period of from five to nine years. A number of chickens, sheep or goats are on free range within the compound. The only method of controlling pests and disease which inflict the yearly crops is to plant at the correct times. The family grows its own food and may or may not have, in addition, trees or arable crops, the produce of which is sold to the local market. This small surplus of produce makes it possible to buy necessities like salt, matches, kerosene for lamps, cloth. If there is plenty of land available, the farm may not expand either because there is no way of selling the surplus crops or because the limit of family help has been reached. The farm is without the services of those of the children who attend the local school.

How should government extension services go about helping? The approach would start with the situation as it is now and build upon what the individual members of the family understand (including the wife or wives who contribute to the tasks of the farm as well as caring for the children and home). The first requisite is for good prices for products, then perhaps credit (in cash or, more likely, in kind); also for new and better quality seeds or seedlings. It is obviously preferable to let the farm carry on in the traditional way with the tasks of clearing, cultivating, weeding, and harvesting, except that an occasion may arise when simple, low-cost improvements could be introduced (if available and well-tried) that would relieve some of the burden of one or more of these operations.

Education in the importance of protein would be part of the help offered and this would be allied to practical suggestions on changes in cropping patterns. At some stage, there may be a case for encouraging commercial poultry keeping, rice production, maize, and crops for factories (from groundnuts to sugar cane, fruit) as justified by the market and the soil. Education could come also through media other than direct confrontation with the district extension worker and his helpers; through mobile vans, radio, newsheets in local languages. Further education again would be provided through mother- and child-care centres.

For the village community as a whole, the mobilizing of self-help through village committees for the creation of inexpensive, local infrastructure – market stalls, feeder roads, drainage systems – is only truly effective if rural leaders include some with training and knowledge of how best the rural community can plan and carry through the tasks involved, with local government providing materials not available locally.

It is not only the lack of capital but also the lack of relevant education (in the wide sense of education) that holds back farm productivity and modest improvements in family living. Here a distinction should be made between education 'for' the rural areas resulting in degrees from universities for those who undertake administration and research, or resulting in diplomas after intermediate-level training for those who work within extensio services in the field; and education 'in' the rural areas where th focus is on the recipients – practising farmers and other rura producers (men and women), workers in co-operatives.

Towards a strategy for rural education

Better quality schooling at lower cost

How can more children, particularly from rural areas, be brought into schools? Can these rural primary schools be made more relevant to the life and work of local communities?

For governments confronting these questions, the most serious constraint is that of finance. Expenditures on primary schooling must compete with resources for other levels of formal education – secondary, technical, and university – and also with resources for strengthening existing and introducing new forms of out-of-school education. Above all, investing greater amounts in primary education (with its relatively long term before yielding dividends) means having less capital now for directly productive activities.

A first approach, perhaps more opportune now than in the 1960s, is to search for *additional* sources of finance for expanding primary education. A guiding principle, well-tested in parts of several countries in tropical Africa, is that families and communities are more willing to contribute towards some purpose which is close at hand and which they value highly. Thus, one proposal is to encourage much greater local contributions, which does not necessarily mean re-introducing or increasing school fees payable by parents. The method of collection will vary according to local acceptability and practice: the imposition may be on families whose children attend schools, or on the entire community in the form of a specific tax, or part of a general levy embracing other local needs. The practice of grants-in-aid from the central government would be initiated or revived with discriminatory procedures to help areas of particularly low (or non-existent) money circulation and to encourage demand where there is little tradition of modern education. On the capital side, thousands of classrooms could be built and maintained by local contributions in money and labour (under the advisory services of central government with specified standards observed). Once again, where the tradition of this kind of self-help does not exist and cannot be made practical, direct intervention by government would be essential.

If primary education is to be improved and expanded – even indeed, by holding to present proportions of school-age children attending schools with populations rising at an annual net increase of around 2.5 per cent – while not retarding other essential development expenditures, drastic policy action on its financing is inevitable. Although the term has wide currency and an understandable appeal, primary schooling can of course neve be 'free'. The problem is to judge correctly the most acceptable and desirable methods for meeting its rising costs.

Decentralising the administration and financing of primary schooling, by strengthening local organization, appears to be a pre-requisite for expansion of other types of education – including out-of-school education activities for post-primary youth and for boys and girls who do not have the opportunity to go to school.

An underlying premise of widespread primary education is it social and economic productivity. In the short run this is no easily proven since the value of schooling experience depend both on the realism of the education provided and on the vitality of the rural economy. In fact, the success of an alliance between rural communities and government in paying for more primary schooling depends heavily on a parallel drive to create more work at higher incomes and arrangements for better living throughout these rural areas.

In line with *the principle that nations of tropical Africa can learn from one another's experience,* a number of examples indicate the possibilities of reducing the unit recurrent cost pe pupil in primary schools.

Introduce double sessions

The problem here is to discover how teachers can teach more pupils without a fall in standards. In parts of Zambia where population density permits, double sessions have been introduced. Most schools have three sessions per day, two for children and one in late afternoon or early evening for adults

Teachers take two of these three sessions each day. Pupils who attend school in the morning receive their work-oriented experience during the afternoon by helping on their family farm plots or within their family compounds. And those who attend school in the afternoon work during the morning.

Make fuller use of expensive teaching staff

Where double sessions are not practical, other ways can be found to make greater use of teachers' time and abilities. Between 85 and 95 per cent of the recurrent cost of primary education is taken up by teachers' salaries; in turn, primary education usually absorbs over half the total expenditures by governments on all formal education. Besides regular daily sessions for children, teachers can be responsible for adult courses in literacy or health education. Again, primary school teachers usually teach for only three-quarters of the year; the remainder of the time, along with their pupils, they are on holiday (around 13 weeks). Besides a leave period, part of this holiday might be spent on refresher courses at teacher training colleges and part in teaching workshop-type courses, such as concentrated literacy classes for young adults.

Share school facilities between children and adults

As a parallel to fuller use of teachers' time, a few countries have multiple purposes for some of their rural schools and thus achieve economies in the use of relatively expensive buildings and equipment. Thus after regular school hours, classrooms are used for demonstrations or lectures by extension services, for adult classes, for community meetings, for the showing of films by mobile units. Tanzania, for example, has abolished the term 'primary schools' and replaced it with 'community education centres', indicating the determination to make fullest use of the facilities.

Introduce alternate-year intake in sparsely-settled areas

Children cannot be expected to walk to school more than a few kilometres especially under a hot sun or in heavy rain. Given this fact, the total possible yearly intake each year to a rural school may be only 20 pupils, whereas the teacher is capable of teaching 40. Several countries, therefore, take in a full class every other year and are thus able to make more efficient use of teachers.

Set a later age for starting school

A number of countries have their children beginning the first class at age 7. Whether the official starting age is 6 or 7, however, numbers of children in all countries start at later ages. There have probably been insufficient experiments to determine an optimum starting age. Preliminary indications are that late starters might be able to accomplish the primary school course in less time and thus at less unit cost. Much would appear to depend, however, on the encouragement to learning provided during the pre-school years.

Provide a four-year primary course for more children

Combined with a later start (from 8 to 10), a primary course of four years would give pupils basic literacy and numeracy. Able ones have the possibility of continuing and later being selected for secondary school. This basic course has advantages over several programmes recently set up in tropical Africa for providing education out-of-school to the standard of UNESCO-defined literacy. In Mali, Tanzania, Ethiopia, for example, adult literacy instruction has been extended to take young people from age 8 to 15. When administrative skills are in short supply (as is almost universally true in tropical Africa today), the running of a supplementary system of education alongside the formal system of primary schooling is probably unduly expensive relative to the quality of the education provided. And young people educated in this way are likely to have little or no chance in the entry competition for secondary schooling.

Reduce the high rate of drop outs

The high rate of dropouts has the effect of reducing the pupil/teacher ratio and thus of raising the recurrent cost per pupil during the upper classes. A higher retention of pupils in schools would not normally increase the layout in public finance, or if it did, only marginally. How can this be achieved? No general formula is possible, only analysis and action at regional and local levels.

Besides reducing unit costs in primary education, two further methods of fund saving have been discussed. Technical education, which is currently provided within government-financed institutes, could be paid for jointly by employers: government and private business. Also, vocational education at the post-primary level can often be as effective, or more effective, when provided on the job, supplemented as required by short courses of a few weeks; this would mean a significant saving.

Apart from questions concerning the economics of education, there are others, equally debated, on the quality of education provided in rural primary schools. Critics of primary education in tropical Africa range widely in their arguments. The systems are inherited, they say, and thus have greater relevance to the industrially-advanced nations of Europe. Primary education is geared to the modern sector of the economy; it creates clerks but divorces children from the realities of their own environment. Methods are out-of-date: stressing the learning of facts rather than the discovery of relationships, encouraging rote imitation rather than innovation. And last, money for education comes from the masses, who are mostly rural and poor, and is used disproportionately to promote the interests of the few.

These are meaningful issues, to be solved by individual nations according to their own patterns of development. More practical, in the present context, is the attention being given to *what* is being taught and *how*. Should special local subjects be taught in rural schools? Children in nomadic Mauritania, for example, are learning to read from an 'urban-oriented' set of primers; here is a case for revising the set to include *both* rural and urban scenes, not only for the identification of children with their own culture but also for the better understanding of other ways of living within the nation.

The suggestion is often made (usually by those with little experience in country areas) that farming or other local vocations should be taught in rural primary schools. Despite the frequency of this recommendation, there is no evidence to show that such teaching will make these young pupils more inclined to appreci- ate rural life nor any more efficient in local occupations. Such vocational learning is likely to be more effective on the job than in the classroom. And the migration of school leavers to the towns and cities will only be reduced when rural life offers in- centives for work with higher incomes.

Pupils who complete the primary course should be able to reac and write fluently in the national language, to solve problems a a certain standard in mathematics, to understand enough science to interpret the world around them, and to have learned suffi- cient history and civics to be aware of their rights and responsi- bilities as citizens of their nation. This does not make pupils intc farmers or government clerks or doctors; it is basic to all these careers. Education is meant not only to adapt pupils to thei society, but also to equip them to alter it. And it may well be that widespread primary schooling provides the foundation fo modernizing agriculture – not by trying to teach pupils to become farmers, but by giving them the tools of literacy and the confidence to try new techniques.

Radical reform in many countries may well be necessary to relate schools more closely to community and national life Subject-content has often been developed in a foreign country very different in its cultural and economic background and, no only that, it is obsolete. In these cases, obviously, new textbook and teaching materials are needed. Language lessons might wel be developed from national life and literature; arithmetic migh include simple accounts using typical farm and market examples science studies would start by analysing elements and relation ships in the familiar environment; geography and history woul begin with reference to the local and national scene. Much more participation in indigenous culture could be encouraged through music, dance, art, folklore. And with these changes in subjec matter, methods of instruction could be improved. The rigid authoritarian manner still used in so many schools to frighten children into rote learning has its counterparts in nineteenth-century Europe and America, but has little justification for being continued in any part of the world today. The newer methods of children learning by participating in discussions and by doing varied operations will have to be infused throughout teacher training colleges. When these reforms are brought about (and in many of the countries of tropical Africa the beginning steps have been taken), then primary schools will become much more vital to the life of local communities – and of the nation.

Yet, whatever alterations are set in motion in the quantity and quality of formal education at the primary (and the secondary) level to accord more accurately with the requirements of the changing society and economy, time is required for them to take place. And there is no sense in planning education that is job-creating and innovative unless parallel efforts are made to reform the economy.

10 Out-of-school a continuing learning experience education:

In recent years interest has quickened in educational activities outside the school system. The first reason is that millions of African children have no access to formal education and these newly-defined programmes appear to offer possibilities for improving abilities on a wide scale at comparatively low cost. And second, for those who have primary schooling these programmes provide the vocational training to smooth the transition from school to work.

One difficulty in using the term 'out-of-school education' is that some of these diverse types of learning actually do go on in schools. 'Non-formal education' is no more accurate since some types are conducted with all the elements present of formal schooling. The term is imprecise, but 'out-of-school education' is taken to mean all those unrelated and unco-ordinated 'sub-systems' whose activities go on in varied settings outside the formal school system. Even with this loose definition, the boundaries are not clear. What begins as an experiment in out-of-school education, perhaps a vocational training centre set up by a voluntary agency, may become absorbed into the formal school system.

Responsibility for the running of out-of-school education is diffuse, consisting of public control (by a variety of ministries of central and local government, statutory corporations, military establishments), private control (by firms, voluntary associations, individuals), or combinations of these.

Methods of instruction vary from the conventional scene of teacher confronting a learning group to the use of radio, demonstrations, mobile training units, visual aids, correspondence courses. Usually there is a high component of learning by doing, particularly in programmes of skill training.

Programmes for the unschooled

One question often posed in this: are there any adequate alternatives to primary schooling, at lower cost and with greater relevance to rural occupations? A number of experiments exist.

Upper Volta: Rural Education Services. This provides a new design of basic education as a substitute for primary schooling in areas where there were no schools. Unschooled youth are admitted from ages 14 to 18 to undergo a three-year, rural-based elementary course in community-built Rural Education Centres. The scheme began in 1961 and by the end of the first decade there were over 700 Centres (including 79 for girls) each with around 45 trainees. (These represented, however, less than one-third the number planned for that date with enrolments one-sixth the proposed total.)

The Centres are administered by a separate organisation within the Ministry of Education, with its own teacher training institutions and inspectorate; syllabuses and instructional aids are centrally designed. Each centre is maintained as a demonstration farm for crop cultivation and livestock management. Additional instruction is given by local extension agents from departments concerned with rural development.

Average annual recurrent costs have been computed as about half the similar costs in a usual primary school. In other respects the experiment is difficult to appraise. Recent reports suggest that although agricultural extension workers are involved, these Centres are not related to market forces and thus provide training isolated from the economic environment.

Mali: Functional Literacy. This programme was designed for those engaged in productive activities between the ages of 15 and 35. At thc start of 1972 over 69,000 were participating in 1,700 Centres. Members help to plan the course which includes literacy in the local language and numeracy and is based on local interests (for example, the operation of scales in weighing produce, the working of co-operatives, the consideration of best sowing dates).

Tanzania: Work-Oriented Adult Literacy Project. This project began in 1968 and by the end of 1971 had 135,000 taking part in 4,500 classes. Its aim is to enable learners (ranging in age from 8 to 45) to reach primary 4 standard in literacy and numeracy and to practice improved farm methods. There are two teaching seasons: the first covers eight months with formal classes six hours a week; the second is a practical period when agricultural staff demonstrate modern farming techniques. Primary 7 school leavers teach and look after libraries for 30/- a month; they are invited to attend community discussion groups on practical subjects.

The goal of this project is for young people and adults to achieve literacy in two years as compared to the four years considered necessary for children in primary schools. This hoped-for objective has not yet been proven on a wide scale nor have comparative costs been analyzed, but the project does have the advantage of lessening the division between illiterate parents and school-going children by making education a community experience. And for children who have no opportunity for schooling, it allows a second chance for gaining literacy.

Malawi: Correspondence College. Malawi children who have reached the fourth grade of primary and are unable to continue further in the school system have been able since 1966 to study through the Malawi Correspondence College. Operating through 62 Correspondence College Centres and 21 evening secondary schools, the College provides upper primary and secondary courses to GCE level for some 15,000 pupils (in 1969). The Centres are used for study group meetings, which are combined with the correspondence courses. In this way many pupils who would otherwise have no such opportunity are able to complete the primary school leaving certificate.

Nigeria: Conversion of Koranic classes to primary schools. As well as founding new primary schools, the Government of Northern Nigeria in 1963 decided to select a number of the widespread Koranic religious schools and enlarge their range of learning to include the disciplines of primary education. *Mallams* were sent to special teacher training colleges to give them methods and materials for teaching the conventional syllabus as well as to improve their Arabic and Islamic background. During the following period some 80 of these Koranic learning groups were reorganized into primary schools with a bias towards Koranic values. Pupils gain work experience after classroom hours by carrying out the customary practical tasks set by the *mallams*. While there is no saving in cost in these converted schools, they are much more closely related to the traditions and values of their communities.

These examples underline how difficult it is to find effective alternatives for primary schools at lower costs. They show, however, the promise of a multi-educational rural centre which serves not only as a primary school, but also as a place for extension demonstrations and films, for work-oriented literacy classes, and for a community library. Some examples also show the possibilities for creating primary schools more in harmony with community activities and values.

Programmes for school leavers

Vocational training for rural school leavers (with full primary education, or nearly so) must necessarily differ in certain respects from that arranged for those who have never been to school. School leavers may not have learned the customary skills which unschooled youth in their age group have mastered through constant practice. And because of 6 to 8 or 10 years in the classroom, they have gained literacy and aspirations often incompatible with rural life. They want to apply themselves to something modern, however vague this ideal in their minds. Although they may be well aware that wage-paid jobs are scarce in the cities, they usually do not see any models for building a life's work in their home areas. The problem of helping school leavers, therefore, is not only to provide vocational training but an associated plan in helping to get them settled in rural occupations.

Where vocational training has a known outcome with wage-paid jobs in modern rural establishments, there has been considerable success. On completing their courses, trainees become extension agents, tractor drivers, mechanics, or technicians in modern processing industries for farm products. But where training is given without being tied to specific jobs with the intention that trainees find opportunities within traditional family farming and other rural small-scale enterprise, there has been only limited success.

The training of school leavers for improved farming, for example, raises important questions. Where should the training be given? In the classrooms of a vocational institute or on the farms? Or some combination of both? Experience in many countries has shown that after long courses in classrooms (with some practical work on farm plots), trainees are often not eager to farm. In some cases, they see the training as a means of further education leading to jobs outside actual farming. In other instances, they may be interested in farming but lack the capital to put into operation what they have learned. A different method of training is for school leavers to start farming on their family land and when they have gained sufficient maturity and practical experience, to receive visits by extension officers. They would also take short courses at the slack period of the farm year in specific practical operations (care of poultry, planting methods for new varieties of seedlings, application of fertilisers). Special groups, such as young farmers' clubs, provide the basis for regular help from extension officers.

Every nation in tropical Africa has a number of programmes for training rural youth – whether by long, short, or intermittent vocational courses or through assistance from extension services. In some areas, voluntary agencies contribute such training programmes along with government services. When compared with the urgent requirements for youth employment and for agricultural progress, the total effort is meagre. Because of shortage of funds and qualified instructors, the choice of type of trainin depends on whether the objective is to help *the few* intensively a relatively high cost or to help *the many* less thoroughly but a lower cost for each individual.

Some examples of rural-training programmes show their variety:

Chad. Eleven centres attached to primary schools provide a two-yea post-primary apprentice training for school leavers ranging in age from 1 to 22 years.

Congo (People's Republic). Young people go to Practical Orientatio Centres for a two-year, part-time practical education related to farmin and small-scale industries (with home economics for girls). This is con pleted by on-the-job training when the youth become engaged in rur occupations.

Ethiopia. The Swedish Evangelical Mission provides a nine-month cours in agriculture and home economics for primary school leavers, whos average age is 18. The trainees do 22 hours a week of practical farmin A recent check on the 65 who had completed the course showed that ove one-half were engaged in farming on their own; one-quarter were withou jobs; and the rest were continuing their education.

Kenya. Village polytechnics provide a two-year training in appropria farming and artisan tasks to primary school leavers who live at home.

Madagascar. Centres for Agriculture and Home Economics provide one-year course combined with work at home. Young men learn abo crop production and animal husbandry; young women take these subjec besides home economics and child care.

Examples of training for improving performances of youn people on the job include:

Botswana. The Brigades provide an unusual approach to on-the-job trai ing in rural skills. In 1965 the Builders' Brigade was started; now the are 31 Brigades with 850 primary school leavers as trainees. The basis the scheme is a three-year work-based training in building, carpentr textiles, tanning, with one day a week of classes devoted to academic an technical education. A major objective is to cover costs of training b undertaking productive work such as contracts to erect buildings, mal furniture, and so on.

oughing with bulls:
improvement
hoe cultivation

12
Tapping rubber in
Western Nigeria

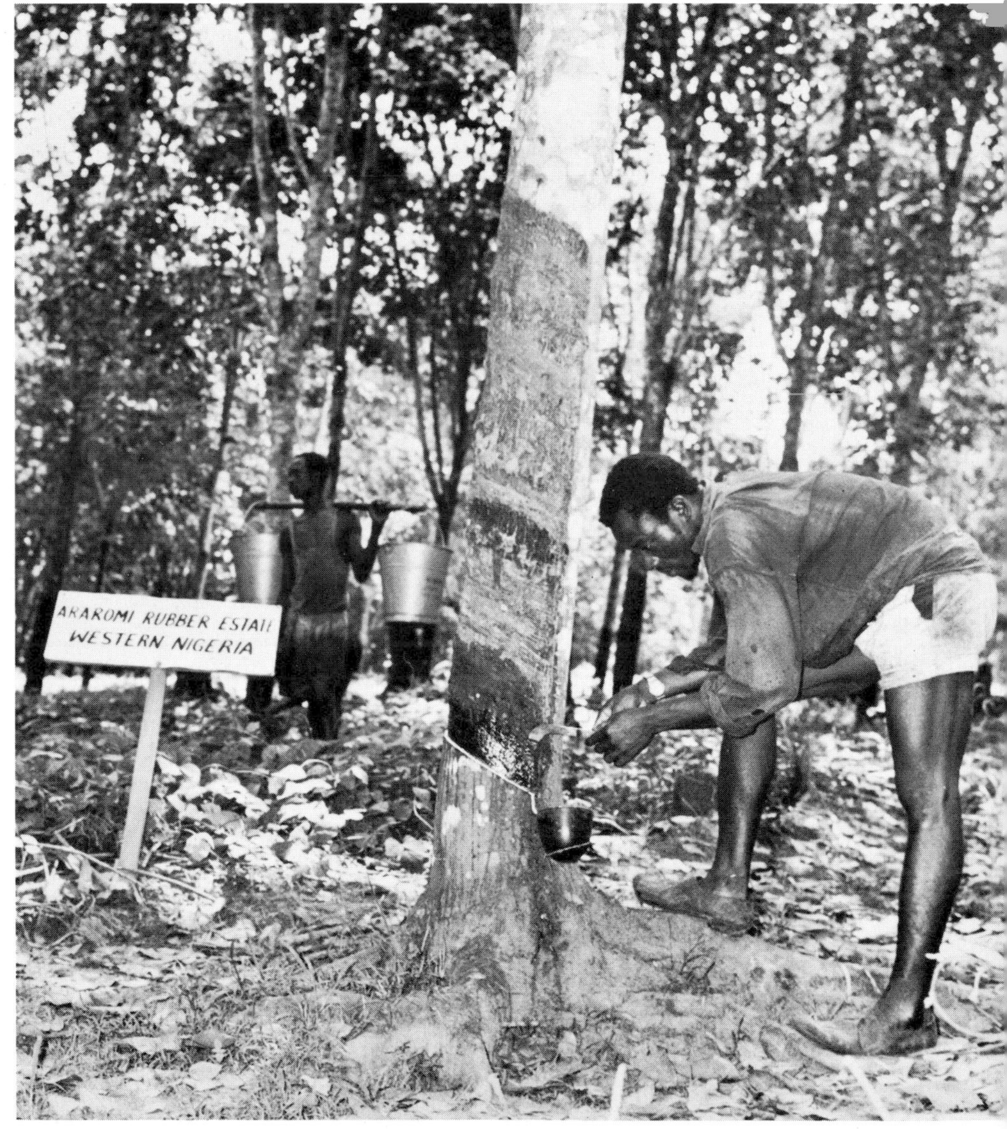

Dahomey: Young Farmers' Clubs, now numbering 125, provide an organization to encourage unschooled youth and early school leavers to mark out land in contiguous plots near their home areas with the assistance of farm extension workers. While living at home, the young farmers clear the land and plant crops. Each mid-day they receive instruction in literacy.

Nigeria. The Faith and Farm agricultural apprenticeship scheme, run by the Church of Christ in the Sudan, places school leavers in a nine-month period of apprenticeship with master farmers (who are normally members of the same Church). Particular emphasis is placed on learning to plough using oxen, and at the end of the apprenticeship the scheme issues each trainee with a bull and plough, plus seeds and fertilisers. His family is expected to match with a contribution of the second bull. The trainee is assisted in obtaining land and is given follow-up support by Faith and Farm.

Nigeria. Twelve Vocational Improvement Centres provide ten-month training courses after regular work hours for lower-grade artisans in industry, government service, and private enterprise. Participants are young adults, mostly with primary education, who have been working in their trades for more than two years. Included also are self-employed artisans and small-business proprietors. Classes are held for two hours each evening 4 or 5 times a week with instruction in general studies (English, arithmetic, book-keeping) and specific technical skills. Trainees are prepared for Government trade tests in motor mechanics, fitting, plumbing, welding, bricklaying, electrical work, painting and decorating, and carpentry.

Uganda. The Nyakashaka Settlement for young farmers is based on crops new to the area. Started in 1963, it has now become a predominantly tea-growing community of over a thousand young farmers, helped by loans to assist in their housing, food, labour, and seedlings.

In addition to these vocational training courses, special training/work programmes for school leavers have been established in a number of the nations of tropical Africa during the 1960s. These programmes have come into being as experimental measures in time of national urgency, and represent a distinct break with the customary methods used for meeting requirements of youth for civic education and specialized training. Most of these national youth service programmes take the trainees away from their homes and enable them to make a disciplined contribution t national development through work projects which may take few months or stretch over a period of one or even two years. I some, the service to the community is through leadership, chiefl in rural areas, after a period devoted mainly to training. Almos all the programmes are rural-oriented. A few only cater fo young women.

Why were these special programmes considered necessary? On commanding reason is the existence of jobless school leavers Another related reason is dissatisfaction with the capacity o ordinary classroom education to produce well-disciplined youth devoted to the nation's cause, who can demonstrate a ne attitude in work and in society.

Examples are: the Zambian Youth Service which provides train ing in general farming activities, the Peoples Republic of th Congo (with its *Action de Rénovation Rurale)* and the Malaw Young Pioneers which include arrangements for agricultura settlement. Training for both farm and non-farm activities i rural areas is provided by the National Youth Service of Keny and the Liberian National Youth Organisation.

For tropical African nations as a whole, however, the total num bers of young people in these national services is not consider-able, not reaching much above 50,000. What is the validity o helping limited numbers at considerable cost in public fund within training/service or training/service/settlement program mes? One answer is that young people engaged in these service later become demonstrators or initiators; they provide leadershi in their home communities; they set examples which make easie the follow-up policies designed to help others. The vast number of young people without the benefits of such training will the have a set of models of what they can aim for.

These programmes are very diverse: differences in age at entry length of education and training, and service periods; in methods of civic education, in the style of community service; in arrangements for settlement later.

On economic grounds, many of the programmes are open to criticism for their high public cost and their diversion of scarce capital and administrative talent from more urgent development tasks.

11 Integrating education within designs for rural development

Rising populations, low economic returns for the majority of rural families, large numbers of unschooled youth, the employment problem of school leavers, excessive migration of rural youth to the cities – these are some of the elements that the nations of tropical Africa are attempting to bring into focus. Success in coping with these difficulties calls for economic reforms.

In these nations prosperous areas are the exception. They are to be found in parts of capital cities and provincial towns and in certain small zones in the countryside, where minerals are being extracted or where high-yielding crops bring good prices. But cases of development do not constitute national economies. The expressed aim of most development plans is that of bringing the products of more family farms into the market economy, of changing rural subsistence living by widening the exchange of goods and services.

Large farm settlement schemes of the 1960s, requiring much capital and not absorbing many people into employment, have not been uniformly successful. Many have not paid their way. This transformation approach has its place in farming (the Gezira scheme, big palm and rubber plantations) but usually there is better economic sense in encouraging existing peasant farms and other small economic units, where output and labour involvement rise almost simultaneously.

What is required are *a great many small but strategic improvements throughout rural economies.* Yet these are proving difficult to bring about. Any one economy has not one environment but many. Planning for substantially more employment along with rising output, and getting these plans into action – within the constraints set by scarce national and local resources – is a difficult, continuing exercise that requires intimate knowledge of people's responses to various familiar and new incentives. Inequalities among areas and even between adjacent communities make administrative decisions about whom to help, and how, extremely complex. The conflict is between the principle of efficiency and the principle of equity in the use of available public resources. Efficiency may well suggest that communities already showing greater motivation and advancement be helped further; equity, that the poorer communities be encouraged to catch up.

Rural communities are usually characterised by closely integrated social systems which include social values, interpersonal relations, and work habits. It is well known that if techniques for local development appear to be imposed from outside they will have little or no chance of achieving their goals. Accordingly, policies and administrative action for getting underway a varied set of improvements over wide areas must correspond with local aspirations.

Designs for integrated rural development include programmes of specialist training, chiefly on the job, for rural producers. Perhaps the most significant innovation in training rural youth and adults is the *multi-purpose rural training centre,* now a well-established feature of East and Central Africa. Here both men and women learn a wide variety of rural skills including farm management, home economics, child care, community development (digging of wells, making of low-cost blocks for building). The centre also provides the setting for the training of extension workers.

The system of formal education (except, in most countries, university education) is the responsibility of the Ministry of Education. Programmes of out-of-school education (and development projects involving education), whether for adults or young people, are arranged and controlled by a variety of ministries, voluntary organisations and firms, or combinations of these. Attaining maximum results at lowest cost in funds calls for *close co-ordination of all activities of rural education within a decentralised learning system:* at central, regional, and district levels.

All countries have their school administrators and extension service officers deployed at different levels. The problem is whether their activities can be co-ordinated more effectively towards the common purpose of rural education. There are obviously many practical difficulties: where the number of field officers is few relative to the tasks at hand, where distances to be covered are vast, where telephones don't usually exist outside the few principal rural centres (and frequently don't function).

Under existing arrangements in most countries, school administrators and extension officers owe loyalty to their particular ministries. This has to be made compatible with the need to consult laterally down the administrative structure to points closest to rural communities. Panels of rural people can co-operate better in two-way communication when their opposite numbers are not separate outside helpers but a group whose activities are being co-ordinated according to the requirements of the local situation. The ideal of *integrated education for rural development* thus requires support by high authority within government and co-ordination at all levels, with extension divisions of departments in continuous consultation among themselves and with local leaders.

Education of young people should be appraised within the perspective of education of every kind available to all members of rural families. At present there would appear to be too exclusiv a concentration on the benefits to be derived from formal school ing for the young, especially at the primary level. The conse quence of this is that out-of-school education in its many forms which reaches more adults and youth, receives insufficient atten tion. Public expenditures on out-of-school education (includin extension services) are presently far outpaced by expenditures o primary schooling.

Apart from programmes of extension in their role of educatin rural populations, what are required are hundreds more smal projects for creating more employment (labour-intensive, self perpetuating, self-multiplying, high in self-help and low in publi cost), that can bring higher money returns to rural communities

Out-of-school education in improved techniques – for farming small-scale industries, and for creating local infrastructure would be a central component in these projects. In the mean time, small wonder that the few isolated innovative training work projects started by governments and voluntary agencie stand out so clearly in the rural areas.

The co-existence of out-of-school learning and formal schoolin means continual pressure on available resources of finance an qualified personnel. It is difficult to see how out-of-schoc education can be expanded without retarding progress in th formal school system. Most nations have made a beginning i low-cost radio broadcasting in local languages as a means o educating rural producers. This is promising, especially in chang ing attitudes and readying people for the demonstrations o extension workers. So, too, are the efforts of mobile teams o educators at work in sparsely populated tracts of the countryside

A further experiment is that of mustering educated people in th rural areas to contribute voluntarily some of their time i providing structured courses in functional literacy.

For the future, a number of important trends can be forecast. They relate to *the transfer of experience of out-of-school education to formal schooling.*

– Greater understanding of the patterns and the value of on-the-job training for rural youth will help in modifying the school curriculum so that it interacts more effectively with subsequent employment of school leavers.

– The farm extension worker and the local agent of public health (and perhaps a successful educated farmer or artisan) have a role, along with the teacher, in the school experience.

– The school itself will be redesigned to become a centre for education of both young and adults and so narrow the gulf in educational attainments among family members. This would also achieve economies of scale in the use of school buildings and educational equipment.

The challenge for the decades remaining of this century is to spread funds and qualified personnel over *a larger community of learners.* A continuous exchange of information, among the nations of tropical Africa, on their educational experiments in school and out of school, could be very helpful — even though many of the innovations are small-scale and specific to particular rural environments; some faltering, others apparently successful. Widening the range of opportunities for work and out-of-school education in the rural areas will not solve the employment problem of rural school leavers. There will still be poor families and poor communities. The movement of people, including the young educated, in search of better work is an important element in economic progress. But at least the worst effects of excessive migration would diminish. Some people from poor rural areas would find work in other more developed rural areas. The employment problem would thus be alleviated in the drive for rural development.

3
earning motor
echanics at
Trade Centre

14
As they work, trainees of the Textile Brigade in Botswana watch the Mechanical Workshop being constructed

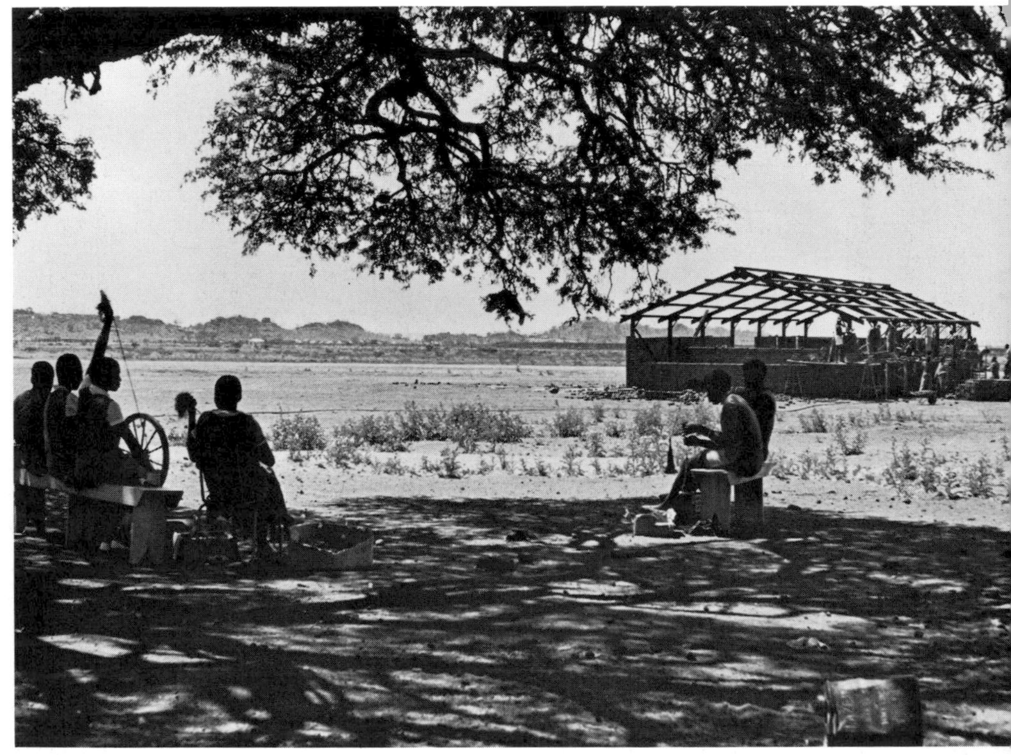

5
uilder's Brigade
ı Botswana

16
Clay Modelling at a Women's Rural Teachers' College

General References

mmonwealth Secretariat, London

Youth and Development in Africa, 1970 (Report of the Commonwealth Africa Regional Youth Seminar, Nairobi, November, 1969)

A. W. Wood, 'Vocational and social training of primary school leavers in African Countries of the Commonwealth'

P. van Rensberg, 'Education and training in relation to rural development'

Education in Rural Areas, 1970 (Report of the Commonwealth Conference on Education in Rural Areas held at the University of Ghana, Legon, Accra, Ghana, March-April, 1970)

R. K. Gardiner, 'Education in rural areas'

L. J. Lewis, 'The school and the rural environment'

F. B. Wilson, 'Education and training for agricultural development'

ernational Institute for Educational Planning, Paris

Planning Out-of-school Education for Development, 1972 (Report of International Seminar held in Paris, December 1971)

erseas Liaison Committee, American Council on Education. Washington DC

Tanzania: A Nation-wide Learning System, 1972 (Report to the Government of Tanzania and the World Bank)

NESCO, Regional Office for Africa, Dakar

Population, Education, Development in Africa, 1971 (Report of meeting of experts held at Dakar, November-December 1971)

Action Training for Development, 1972 (Report of Round Table on An Alternative Education for Youth? held at Dakar in February 1972)

ited Nations, New York

Report on Children, 1971

NICEF, Paris

Assignment Children, Numbers 1 to 20

orld Health Organization, Geneva

'Nutrition: Key to Development' in *Justice and Service* (World Council of Churches Newsletter No. 1, 1972)

Economic Commission for Africa, Addis Ababa

Annual Report 1970-71, Volume 1

Food and Agricultural Organization, Rome

World Conference on Agricultural Education and Training, Report, 1970

African Rural Employment Study, Rural Employment Paper No. 1

D. Byerlee and C. K. Eicher, *Rural Employment, Migration an Economic Development: Theoretical Issues and Empirical Evidence fror Africa* (Department of Agricultural Economics, Michigan State Univer sity, East Lansing, Michigan, September 1972)

Population, Urbanization, Area, Density

	Total Populations 1970	1980 (millions)	Population living in towns of + 20,000 inhabitants (per cent)	Area in sq. km. (thousand)	Density per sq. km.
Botswana	.6	.8	22	600	1
Burundi	3.6	4.6	2	27	129
Cameroon	5.8	7.3	7	475	12
Central African Republic	1.5	1.9	16	622	2
Chad	3.7	4.8	7	1,284	3
Congo (People's Republic)	.9	1.2	10	342	3
Dahomey	2.7	3.6	12	112	24
Equatorial Guinea	.28	.33	33	28	10
Ethiopia	25.0	31.5	5	1,221	20
Gabon	.48	.54	11	267	2
Gambia	.36	.45	10	11	32
Ghana	9.0	12.6	17	238	38
Guinea	3.9	5.0	11	245	16
Ivory Coast	4.3	5.6	19	322	13
Kenya	10.9	15.1	8	582	19
Lesotho	1.0	1.3	2	30	34
Liberia	1.1	1.4	18	111	11
Madagascar	6.9	9.3	10	587	12
Malawi	4.4	5.8	4	118	37
Mali	5.1	6.6	7	1,240	4
Mauritania	1.2	1.5	2	1,030	1
Mauritius	.9	1.1	47	2	421
Niger	3.8	5.2	4	1,267	3
Nigeria	66.2	87.6	15	923	72
Rwanda	3.6	4.8	0	26	136
Senegal	3.9	5.1	27	196	20
Sierra Leone	2.6	3.4	13	71	37
Somalia	2.8	*3.6	12	637	4
Swaziland	.42	.57	5	17	24
Tanzania	13.2	17.5	6	939	14
Togo	1.9	2.5	10	56	33
Uganda	8.6	11.3	5	236	36
Upper Volta	5.4	6.8	4	274	20
Zaïre	21.6	27.8	15	2,345	9
Zambia	4.3	5.9	24	752	6

Table 2

Population Growth, Infant Mortality, Dependency (around 1969)

	Birth and death rates per 1,000 inhabitants		Annual rate of demo-graphic growth	Number of years for the population to double	Infant mortality rate: death under 1 year old per 1,000 live births	Populatio unde 15 years ol
	Death	Birth	(per cent)			(per cent
Botswana	—	—	2.0	35	—	4[illegible]
Burundi	46	26	2.0	35	150	4[illegible]
Cameroon	50	27	2.2	32	137	3[illegible]
Central African Republic	48	30	1.7	41	190	4[illegible]
Chad	45	31	1.5	47	160	4[illegible]
Congo (People's Republic)	41	24	1.7	41	—	—
Dahomey	54	26-31	2.9	24	110	4[illegible]
Equatorial Guinea	—	—	—	—	—	—
Ethiopia	—	—	2.0	35	—	—
Gabon	35	30	0.9	78	229	3[illegible]
Gambia	39	19	2.1	33	—	3[illegible]
Ghana	47	20	2.5	28	156	4[illegible]
Guinea	55	35	2.0	35	216	44
Ivory Coast	56	33	3.3	31	—	43
Kenya	50	20	3.0	23	132	46
Lesotho	40	23	1.8	39	181	4[illegible]
Liberia	40	—	1.8	39	—	37
Madagascar	46	22-25	2.4	29	102	46
Malawi	—	—	2.5	28	—	4[illegible]
Mali	52	30-32	2.0	35	123	49
Mauritania	45	25-28	2.0	35	107	—
Mauritius	30	9	2.0	35	65	44
Niger	52	25-27	2.7	26	200	4[illegible]
Nigeria	50	25	2.5	28	—	43
Rwanda	52	—	2.7	26	137	—
Senegal	43	17	2.5	28	93	42
Sierra Leone	44	22	2.2	32	146	37
Somalia	—	—	3.1	23	—	—
Swaziland	36	—	2.9	24	—	—
Tanzania	43	23	2.9	24	189	42
Togo	55	29	2.6	27	127	48
Uganda	42	20	2.5	28	160	4[illegible]
Upper Volta	53	35	2.0	35	182	42
Zaïre	43	20	2.3	31	104	39
Zambia	51	20	3.1	23	259	45

School Enrolment Ratios

	School-age Children in Schools (per cent) 1970		Female Enrolments as Percentage of Total Enrolments 1970	
	Primary	Secondary	Primary	Secondary
Botswana	56	8	53	44
Burundi	24	2	31	25
Cameroon	68	8	43	27
Central African Republic	57	3	32	19
Chad	21	2	24	7
Congo (People's Republic)	87	17	44	29
Dahomey	31	5	32	29
Equatorial Guinea	68	17	41	37
Ethiopia	13	3	30	23
Gabon	91	14	48	29
Gambia	25	11	31	24
Ghana	61	21	44	32
Guinea	26	10	31	20
Ivory Coast	49	10	36	21
Kenya	54	9	41	28
Lesotho	65	7	60	54
Liberia	30	9	30	23
Madagascar	55	9	46	39
Malawi	31	2	—	—
Mali	19	5	36	22
Mauritania	12	2	28	8
Mauritius	93	27	48	39
Niger	12	1.2	34	25
Nigeria	32	3	39	29
Rwanda	55	2	43	33
Senegal	33	8	38	26
Sierra Leone	30	8	40	29
Somalia	8	3	24	16
Swaziland	54	16	49	44
Tanzania	29	2	—	—
Togo	52	7	31	23
Uganda	31	4	38	24
Upper Volta	10	1.3	35	25
Zaïre	61	9	36	23
Zambia	71	11	44	33

Source for Tables 1, 2 & 3: UNESCO Regional Office for Africa, Dakar
'—': data not available

Out-of-school and Formal Education of Young People for Rural Employment in Tropical Africa

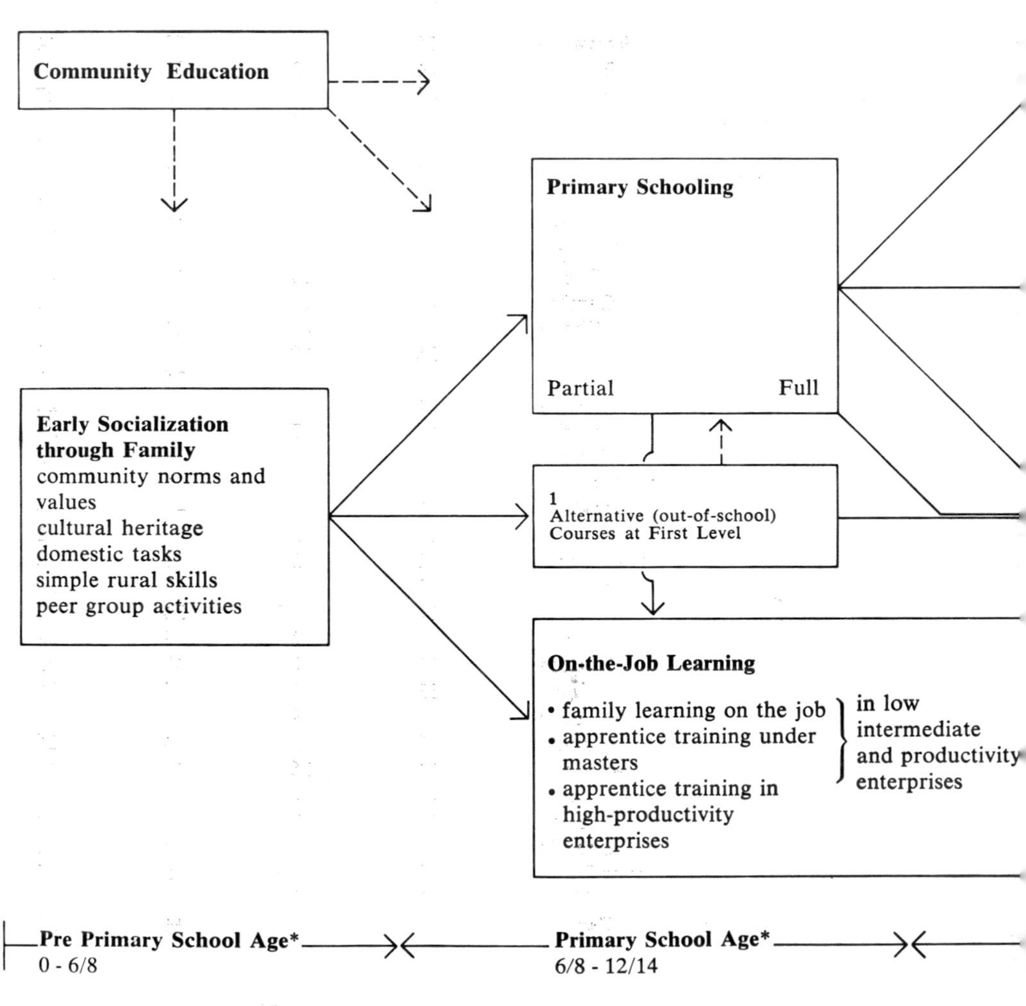

* Boys and Girls

1 For numeracy, literacy, civic education, simple vocational skills recreation, cultural activities

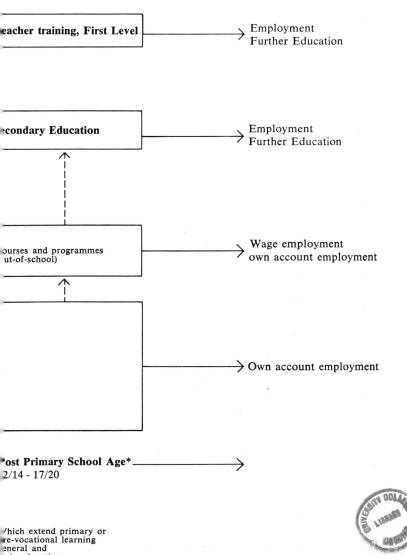

eacher training, First Level → Employment
Further Education

:condary Education → Employment
Further Education

ourses and programmes
ut-of-school) → Wage employment
own account employment

→ Own account employment

'ost Primary School Age* →
2/14 - 17/20

/hich extend primary or
re-vocational learning
eneral and
vic education
re-vocational learning
ocational skills